COPING WITH COT DEATH

SARAH MURPHY grew up in Northumberland but now lives in Sussex. She is married with three children. Her career experiences include social work, playgroup supervision and teaching, but she now works as part-time secretary to her husband Pat and divides her remaining time between her family and her two main hobbies of writing and riding. *Coping With Cot Death* is a direct result of the cot death in 1979 of Elizabeth, one of Pat and Sarah's 3 month old twin daughters.

Overcoming Common Problems Series

Overcoming Common Problems Series

Overcoming Common Problems Series

Overcoming Common Problems

COPING WITH COT DEATH

Sarah Murphy

SHELDON PRESS
LONDON

First published in Great Britain in 1990
Sheldon Press, SPCK, Marylebone Road, London NW1 4DU

British Library Cataloguing in Publication Data
Murphy, Sarah
    Coping with cot death. – (Overcoming common problems).
    1. Sudden infant death syndrome
    I. Title. II. Series
    082306.88

ISBN 0–85969–606–5

Photoset by Deltatype Ltd, Ellesmere Port, Cheshire
Printed in Great Britain by Biddles Ltd, Guildford and Kings Lynn

Contents

To Elizabeth

I am very grateful for the help given by my family, friends, the Foundation (especially Dr Richard Wilson; Erica De'Ath, the Chief Executive; Silvia Limerick, the Vice Chairman; and June Reed, the secretary, for their information and advice), health and welfare professionals and all bereaved families who so kindly agreed to share their experiences and contribute to the book.

Before you read this book. . .

If, like me, you tend to skip the Foreword in books, I hope I can persuade you to read what follows because it will give me a chance to explain the term 'cot death' and to describe briefly what the book is about and why it has been written. The book is for many different people – for families trying to cope after the sudden and unexpected death of their baby or young child . . . for relatives, friends and professionals wanting to know how best to help . . . for families worried that their baby may be at risk of cot death and wanting to learn as much as possible in order to try and prevent such a death from happening . . . for Elizabeth, our little daughter who died at the age of 3 months, in memory of her and as a tribute to her . . . for myself, as one way of trying to come to terms with her death.

It is natural to fear the unknown and cot death is still an unknown, a tragic and baffling mystery waiting to be solved. It therefore takes courage to decide to read a book about it, because doing so acknowledges cot death as a reality and we all wish that it did not exist. Many of us know only too well that it does, but for anyone prepared to read about it without ever having experienced it, learning more about cot death does not mean that it will happen to you. Buying this book does not mean that your baby or a baby known to you will 'catch' cot death in some way – on the contrary, since the proceeds are being donated to research you will be doing something positive to safeguard your own and other people's babies, for it is only through research that the answers to the mystery will be found. We owe it to all those babies who have died, as well as to all those now living and yet to be born, to ensure that these answers are found and future deaths prevented.

Confusion sometimes arises between the terms 'cot death' (known in America as 'crib death') and 'sudden infant death syndrome'. Deaths registered as sudden infant death syndrome are also cot deaths, but not all cot deaths can be correctly described as sudden infant death syndrome (SIDS). This is because cot death was the term originally used in 1954 to describe the sudden and unexpected death of an apparently healthy baby. In cot deaths the subsequent post-mortem sometimes finds an explanation, though in the majority only a partial explanation is found and in some, no

1

explanation at all is found. SIDS has been used since 1969 to describe those deaths which are sudden and unexpected by history (that is, the baby's state of health before hand) and for which no adequate cause can be found, even after a thorough post-mortem – in other words, cot deaths which are partially or wholly unexplained.

Coping With Cot Death is based on my own experiences and responses and also on those of the many families with whom I have been in contact in the years since our daughter's death. When our baby daughter died in 1979, I felt a great need to learn as much as possible about cot death, but it was difficult to find any information on the subject. The book begins, therefore, by examining all the facts currently known about cot death, with suggestions about possible means of prevention. It then focuses on how different members of a family bereaved by a cot death are likely to be affected by their grief, with advice on how best to try and cope. (If you find the first chapter too dry because it has so many facts and statistics, it might be more helpful to read the chapters concerned with feelings first and return to the opening chapter later, when the time seems right.) It offers guidance on how to deal with the practical necessities which follow a baby's sudden death, it looks in detail at who can help and how best they can do so and it offers information, guidance and advice for bereaved parents wondering whether to risk having another baby. It includes a list of useful addresses and a list of leaflets, books and videos, so that bereaved families and those wanting to help them can know exactly what information and support is available. It is the culmination of all that I have experienced and learnt in the ten years since our daughter's death. I hope it will help.

1
Cot Death – the Facts

What is 'cot death'?

In 1969 the sudden infant death syndrome (or SIDS, which we tend to call 'cot death' and which Americans tend to call 'crib death') was defined in America by Dr Beck as: 'The sudden death of any infant or young child which is unexpected by history and in which a thorough post-mortem examination fails to demonstrate an adequate cause of death.' That is the medical definition and it describes the condition, but not the starkness of the tragedy which it creates. The nightmare reality which all cot-death parents have to face is that when they last check on their baby they find that all is well and when they next check, they find their baby dying or dead. No warning, no hint of anything significantly wrong beforehand, no explanation afterwards, just the unacceptable finality of sudden death.

It seems incredible to parents, but SIDS has only been accepted as a registerable cause of death in the UK since 1971 and included in the International Classification of Diseases since 1979. It is therefore only in recent years that the number of such deaths has been recorded with any degree of accuracy. It seems unlikely that cot deaths are on the increase, simply that they appear to be so as they become more recognized and as other causes of death are gradually prevented.

Sudden death in infancy has existed since biblical times. Solomon's judgment concerning the two mothers disputing parenthood of the surviving infant is a prime example (1 Kings 3). In those times it was believed that the baby must have been accidentally lain on in bed during the night and so died of suffocation. This belief of overlaying as the cause of death in such cases persisted for thousands of years, causing deep anguish for the many families involved. Now, at least, more is known about the condition because of research and, as a result, a number of false theories, including that of overlaying, have been eliminated. Overlaying was finally disproved as a cause when fashions in babycare changed. Parents began to lay their infants in cots at night instead of allowing them to share the parental bed. Instead of reducing once overlaying was no

3

longer a possibility, the rate of sudden infant deaths which could not be explained remained constant. The current view is that there are probably several causes and that death could be due to a combination of factors coming together at a vulnerable period of development.

The tragedy of cot death is worldwide, but in many countries it is difficult to obtain accurate figures. It is more common in countries such as the UK, USA and Australia than in countries such as Finland and Sweden. In Britain the rate (the average number of deaths occurring per 1,000 live births) is about 2.3 per 1,000. In North America it is also about 2.3 per 1,000 and in Australasia it ranges from 1.6 to 4.1. Sweden, by contrast, has a rate of only about 0.6 per 1,000, and for some reason the Jewish areas of Israel also have a very low incidence. In highly advanced countries, SIDS is now recognized to be the most common kind of death in babies aged between 1 week and 1 year. In some places it is more common at the age of 3 months than all other causes of death combined.

Each year between 1,000 and 2,000 babies in this country under the age of 2 die suddenly, for no obvious reason, and that means more than thirty babies every week, or on average five babies every day. Of the babies who die, 40 per cent are aged between 2 and 4 months, and 90 per cent of all cot deaths take place before the age of 8 months. Although the remaining 10 per cent is a small proportion, these children can die at any time up until they are 2 years old. The deaths of SIDS babies less than 1 month and over 6 months in age occur relatively evenly through the year, while those aged between 1 and 6 months tend to die more often during the winter months, suggesting that infection may play a part. The rate of SIDS varies from 1.5 per 1,000 live births in babies born in March to 2.6 for those born in October.

For those who find graphs a helpful way of interpreting statistics, three are reproduced here. Fig. 1 shows the age in weeks reached by 279 baby girls who died in cot deaths between the ages of 1 week and 1 year. Fig. 2 shows a similar graph for 417 baby boys, and in both graphs the peak ages show very clearly. Fig. 3 shows the time of year at which cot deaths occurred. The winter peak shows very clearly.

As many babies die during the day as during the night. SIDS is slightly more common in boys than in girls. It is more common in twins, in low birth-weight or premature babies and in babies whose mothers are young, smoke and have had a number of previous children. With single babies the risk of a cot death is 1 in 500 live

4

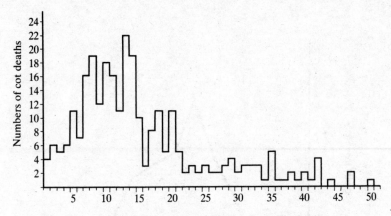

Fig. 1. Age in weeks of 279 female cot deaths

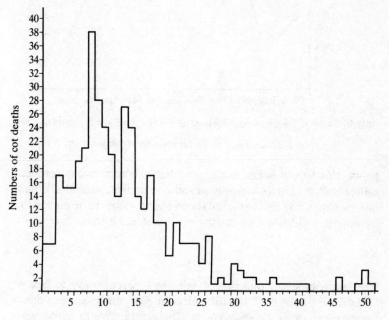

Fig. 2. Age in weeks of 417 male cot deaths

births. With twins or triplets a cot death is two or three times more likely, with the ratio rising from 2 to 4 or 6 per 1,000 live births. Part of this may be accounted for by the fact that multiple-birth babies tend to be premature and of low birth-weight, two significant risk factors. Since the risk is the same in both identical and non-identical

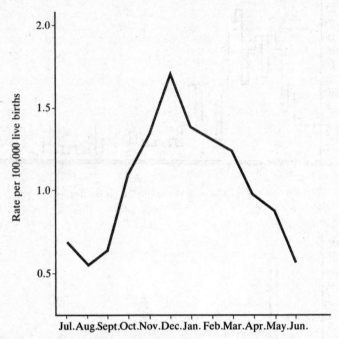

Fig. 3. Seasonal Distribution of 2891 cot deaths (England and Wales 1979–80–81)

(Figs 1–3 reproduced by kind permission of Lady Limerick)

twins, this would seem to suggest that a common environment rather than a genetic factor is to some extent responsible. Where one twin dies, the risk to the surviving twin appears to be high in the month after the co-twin's death, but thereafter it falls.

Why?

The one compelling question all cot-death parents have to face is: 'Why did my baby die?' It is difficult enough trying to accept a death for which there is a known cause. To be told: 'We're sorry, your beautiful and apparently healthy baby (or child) has died but we can't give you any reason,' makes trying to accept the death almost impossible.

The need to know often becomes a driving force for bereaved parents, giving them the courage to ask questions and to seek out possible theories. Because the need to know is so great, this chapter will concentrate on an examination of the various theories which exist. Inevitably this means that the chapter may seem very dry and technical in places, so if you do not feel able to cope with an array of facts at the moment, you may prefer to read some of the other chapters first and return to this one later.

Every time a new theory is suggested, it is very tempting for cot-death parents to seize upon it and try to make it relate to their own particular case, like one of Cinderella's sisters desperately trying to squeeze her foot into a shoe that refuses to fit. There is no shortage of such theories. The newspapers seem only too willing to publish them (with or without supporting scientific evidence) and they are sometimes known as the 'flavour of the month' theories because they change and replace each other so often.

When no theories seem relevant, the logical response for parents is to grope around trying to find one of their own. I had just painted a toy cupboard the day before Elizabeth died. On the evening before her death she had been in the lounge, close to possible paint fumes, so I tried to convince myself that they must have played a part in her subsequent death. Remembering that cot deaths have existed for thousands of years can help when the temptation arises to blame a modern invention or circumstance.

It is very understandable that, since no reason is apparent, we feel the need to find one no matter how unlikely it may be. I don't know if it is true, but I remember being told about one mother who had always put on her baby's nappy in a certain way. Just before his death she had switched to a different method, so that when he did die totally unexpectedly, she became convinced that her new method of fastening the nappy must have been to blame. The need to find a reason is very compelling and this is well recognized by the Foundation for the Study of Infant Deaths.

What causes cot death?

In 1971 the Foundation for the Study of Infant Deaths was formed with three aims: to raise funds for research, to support bereaved families and to act as a centre for information. Its work in all three areas has been invaluable. In trying to identify causes and ways of prevention it has raised very large sums of money and has sponsored over 100 research projects. It is generally agreed that there is no single cause of all cot deaths and that it is probably a 'multi-factorial' condition – in other words, that there are a number of 'stresses', possibly trivial in themselves, but lethal when they come together at a critical time in the baby's development. Some factors are now well documented – prematurity and low birth-weight are known to increase the risk, sleep behaviour and the age of the infant appear to be relevant to many deaths and over half the babies concerned have some form of infection, however slight, usually of the respiratory tract. In his helpful book *Sudden Death in Infancy – The 'cot death' syndrome,* published in 1983, Professor Bernard Knight has suggested that SIDS is 'a final common pathway, almost certainly via respiratory failure leading to heart failure and this pathway can be reached by a number of different routes'. This sequence of events, however, is not yet proven.

Many areas have been researched. For parents like ourselves, the medical terms which have to be used when reporting such research projects can seem very difficult and daunting, but most of us are prepared to struggle with them because of our overwhelming need to know. Here is a list of some of the main areas in which research has taken place (if you would like to examine these in detail or to consider others I would recommend you to the book mentioned above and especially to the excellent and very thorough and comprehensive book, *Sudden Infant Death – Patterns, Puzzles and Problems* by Jean Golding, Sylvia Limerick and Aidan Macfarlane, published in 1985 by Open Books):

(1) Breathing patterns and reflexes
(2) Heart rates and rhythms
(3) Heart conduction defects
(4) Sleep apnoea (absence of breathing) and its connection with (1) and (2)
(5) Allergy to cow's milk
(6) Allergy to house mites
(7) Viral infection
(8) Bacterial infection
(9) Botulism
(10) Failure of the immune system
(11) Hyperthermia (overheating)
(12) Hypothermia (low temperature)
(13) Malignant hyperpyrexia
(14) Carbon-dioxide pooling
(15) Stress
(16) Carbon-monoxide poisoning
(17) Errors of metabolism

(18) Internal mechanical obstruction to breathing
(19) External mechanical obstruction to breathing
(20) Abnormal lung surfactant
(21) Low calcium levels/laryngeal spasm
(22) Hypernatraemia (high sodium in the blood)
(23) Hypoglycaemia (low levels of blood sugar)
(24) Thyroid-hormone imbalances
(25) Deficiency of trace elements
(26) Vitamin deficiency
(27) Biotin deficiency
(28) Thiamine deficiency
(29) Infanticide (very infrequent and believed to be only responsible for 1 per cent of all unexplained baby deaths)

Some of the research is beginning to provide explanations for small proportions of cot deaths. An inherited enzyme (MCAD) deficiency has been found in about 7 per cent of cot-death babies, in whom death may have been triggered by infection. MCAD stands for Medium Chain Acyl CoA Dehydrogenase. It is one of 15 enzymes in the body concerned with fatty acid oxydation. The lack of this enzyme prevents the normal breakdown of fatty acids and so the usual energy reserves are not then available. (The body has to convert fat into glucose at times of stress such as when coping with an infection.) In some parts of the USA about 4 per cent of sudden infant deaths are due to infant botulism, which was only first identified in 1976. A great deal is being learned about the physiological development of infants and how infection and temperature may alter breathing and heart-rate patterns. Some theories, of course, are found to have no validity once they have been researched. A possible association between routine immunization and subsequent cot death was investigated, for example, but no evidence was found and it was felt that the only association must be one of time – immunization commences at around 3 months and cot deaths peak at around 3 months. Having said that, there has been the suggestion that whooping cough itself may cause some deaths, with such deaths occurring before it has developed into the obvious form and therefore before it could be detected.

Because of research, some very important questions have been resolved and some very interesting findings have been discovered along the way. If your instincts as parents tell you that something might be involved which has not yet been researched, do contact the

Foundation and let them know. They will not think you foolish, no matter how unlikely your theory might appear to be, and if enough parents were to contact them with coinciding theories, an important factor might emerge.

Where minor illnesses are concerned, respiratory viral infections stand out because of the frequency with which they coincide with SIDS. In Britain respiratory syncytial virus is the major cause of admission to hospital for respiratory disease in children under 5. The viral infection certainly has definite parallels with SIDS: the most common age at admission is between 1 and 3 months; the most common occurrence is in babies living in cities; the least common occurrence is in babies of social class I; the ratio of boys to girls is 1.4 to 1 (identical to that for SIDS); the children who suffer from the respiratory syncytial virus tend to have older brothers and sisters and the viral infection occurs most frequently during the winter months (the peak time of year for SIDS). Of course, it is possible that studies of other viral infections would reveal a similar pattern and, as research techniques become more sophisticated, evidence of other previously undetected viral infections may be found.

Minor illnesses do seem to play a recurring part in the pattern presented by SIDS, perhaps adding an extra stress to the baby at a time when he or she is possibly especially vulnerable because of other causes. As mentioned earlier, SIDS is thought to be multi-factorial. In our daughter Elizabeth's case, she was already carrying two high-risk factors because of her prematurity and the fact that she was a twin. When she died at the peak age of 3 months, she was suffering from a sticky eye and also, I suspect, from a throat or larynx infection, since her voice had changed on the day before she died and at one stage she had become very croaky, almost to the point of losing her voice completely. Both these conditions, though minor in themselves, may have contributed in some way.

On the night before she died, she was given a bottle-feed of formula milk instead of her usual breast milk because my supply had run short and she seemed to be very hungry. Although she had received some formula milk whilst on the Special Care Baby Unit without any apparent adverse affect, on the whole she had been almost totally breastfed. Her twin sister Mary later showed signs of being allergic to cow's milk protein, just like our older daughter Rebecca. It could well be that allergy to cow's milk protein also played a part. In addition, Elizabeth had a tendency to become overheated and sweat much more than her twin Mary, even when they were wearing identical clothes, using the same sheets and blankets and sharing the same twin pram. It could be that this tendency also resulted in one more stress factor and that it was the combination of all these stress factors at a critical time which proved fatal. It is something which we can never know for certain, but instinct tells me that overheating played a part and perhaps it is relevant that our surviving twin did not have to cope with that problem, nor was she fighting two minor infections at the critical age of 3 months.

New and more sophisticated areas of research are being opened up all the time. For those of you willing to tackle the medical terms involved, some of the most recent projects in 1989 include:

(a) A study of 'chemo-reflex'. Most cot-death babies die quietly in their sleep, which suggests a poor chemo-reflex. Chemo-reflex is a change in function brought about by chemical substances. The study aims to examine whether this is indeed the case and to define how the chemo-reflex matures in babies.
(b) The application of a new and very sensitive and specific technique for diagnosing infection – in-situ DNA hybridization – which will be able to find viral nucleic acid in lung tissue and identify the nature of the virus.
(c) A study of apnoea (absence of breathing) in the upper airway chemo-reflex (UACR) to examine how the UACR matures in infants and whether it is different in light or deep sleep.
(d) An investigation of growth in cot-death babies, using records of 350 SIDS babies in Oxfordshire and West Berkshire and matching these with records of 1,050 controls from the same region.
(e) In the March 1989 issue of the *British Medical Journal*, the finding of significantly greater amounts of immunoglobulin (antibody) in the lungs of SIDS infants compared with control infants was reported from Australia. This could suggest an abnormal immunological response to a minor infection (an area being investigated in Projects 87 and 105). It might even represent an acute allergic happening in the lung and this area is being investigated in Project 95.

If you are able to gain access to copies of the *British Medical Journal* it is often a useful source of information about cot death. The March 1989 issue quoted above discussed the possible role played by hypoxia (lack of oxygen). It also queried whether laying babies on their tummies could be a risk factor, since the face is an important cooling source and keeping the face next to the mattress might increase the risk of hyperthermia (overheating). In the Netherlands, where there has been a growing trend of laying babies on their tummies, there has been a three-fold increase in SIDS since 1971. In the light of this, it might seem sensible to lay your baby on his or her side rather than the tummy, with a rolled-up sheet or blanket tucked behind as a support. It might also be sensible to be cautious about the use of baby bonnets, as these prevent the baby's head from acting as a natural cooling source. Whilst bonnets may certainly be needed when the baby is outside on a cold day, they should always be removed once the baby is back inside a warm house again or travelling inside a warm car.

Can cot death be prevented?

Some of the positive steps which may help to prevent cot death and which can be taken by any couple planning to have a baby are outlined in Chapter 8. In addition to these, the following are all considered to be possible preventive measures:

Monitors

One of the most consistent hypotheses to be considered in cardio-respiratory research is the possible role played by sleep apnoea – prolonged interruptions in the baby's breathing which it is suggested could lead to fatal oxygen deficiency and respiratory depression culminating in cardio-respiratory failure (in other words, ceasing of the breathing and heartbeat). The evidence so far neither proves nor disproves this theory. It may be relevant to a proportion but not to all cot deaths. It could perhaps, however, be prevented in two ways: by finding out the underlying cause of apnoea or by recognizing it in time to break the downward spiral, either by constant twenty-four hours-a-day watching (which is not feasible for parents) or by use of an effective apnoea monitor. The two most well-known current models are the Graseby MR10 and the Eastwood Eastleigh 200. The Graseby works by means of a small sensor pad which is attached to the baby's tummy by micropore tape and linked by a thin cord to a small 'box' called a monitor. The pad is sensitive to the baby's breathing movements. If breathing ceases for more than a specifically set length of time (ten or twenty seconds) the alarm sounds and a red light flashes. The Eastleigh monitor works by means of a flat pressure-sensitive sensor pad which is placed under the baby's mattress. As with the Graseby, each breath taken is indicated by an audible 'click' and a light indication. After a lapse in breathing of ten, fifteen or twenty seconds (depending on the pre-set alarm period) a loud alarm and a red light are activated. Another monitor, the Densa, operates in a similar way but with this monitor, a specially designed elasticated strap containing the sensor pad fastens around the baby's body and can be worn over normal outdoor clothing.

Unfortunately existing apnoea monitors are not designed to detect obstructive apnoea and they may fail to detect central apnoea reliably. At the moment, an apnoea alarm may fail to sound because it confuses heart beat and breathing or because it registers, quite correctly, that the abdomen or chest is still moving (that is, that the baby's tummy is still moving up and down as with normal breathing) even though the upper airway is blocked and airflow has ceased.

In January 1985 a report was issued called: *Apnoea Monitors and SID* – Milner (Archives of Disease in Childhood, Vol. 60, No. 1, 76–80). It is available from the Foundation. The report examined the four types available at the time – the Graseby Dynamics MR10 Respiration Monitor; the Vickers Apnoea Alarm Mark 3; the Eastwood RE 134 Apnoea Monitor/Eastleigh Apnoea Respiration Monitor RE22, and the impedance systems – but concluded: 'An ideal monitor should 1) Reliably identify cessation of respiratory air flow including obstructive apnoea 2) Have no alarms at times when the baby is breathing adequately 3) Incorporate a data-storage system so that information can be retrieved about events preceding an alarm. None of the systems commercially available in the UK fulfils any of these criteria.' Since 1985 monitors have been invented which can detect low levels of oxygen tension in the skin, or measure oxygen saturation, and these are currently undergoing trials.

Even if a foolproof, inexpensive apnoea monitor does become available, there is no final evidence that it will be a preventive measure for SIDS, but on the other hand the monitors which are available at the moment, despite their limitations, are known to give great comfort and reassurance to cot-death parents caring for subsequent babies, and the 1985 report did accept that such monitors do have a place in highly selected situations.

Weighing scales

Weighing scales give visible proof that the baby is gaining weight and thriving and they have a useful role to play provided that they are used regularly in the home under consistent conditions (that is, at the same time of day, before a feed, with the baby unclothed or wearing exactly the same weight of clothing each time) and provided that the results are then plotted on a special chart known as the Sheffield Weight Chart. These special charts are available from the Foundation and they are designed to indicate clearly if any cause for concern arises regarding the weight of the baby. It is known, for example, that sudden weight losses often precede illness and daily weighing has been known to detect the very early stages of potentially serious illnesses such as kidney infections. Since rapidly developing viral infections still have not been ruled out as a possible cause of cot death, weighing scales could well have a relevant part to play in the fight against the syndrome, provided, of course, that any significant weight loss is followed up immediately by the health visitor or doctor and appropriate medical attention given to the baby concerned.

For those who wish to know more about the use of monitors and/ or weighing scales, these are both discussed in further detail in Chapter 8 (see pp. 113–15).

Scoring systems

Although there is at the present no definite way of predicting or preventing SIDS, the devising of 'scoring systems' for babies thought to be at increased risk has produced encouraging results. Work carried out in Sheffield, where extra attention was given to 'at risk' babies, resulted in a lowering of the rate of cot deaths from 5.2 in 1972 to 1.9 in 1978/9. In July 1984 an ITV programme called *The Purple Line* also drew attention to this aspect of preventive work which had been taking place in Sheffield and in Gosport, Portsmouth. The implication from the studies was that better health care could help to prevent some deaths and perhaps it is no coincidence that in Finland, which has a high standard of both ante-and post-natal care, the incidence of cot deaths is very much lower than in our own country.

Two scoring systems exist at the moment in the UK – the Sheffield Multistage Scoring System and a refined and modified system devised by the Foundation. A cot death becomes known as a SID (sudden infant death) if no adequate cause of death is discovered at post-mortem. The Sheffield system was devised in relation to all unexpected deaths (including ones where a cause was subsequently identified), so perhaps the more accurate system is the one devised by the Foundation and which is reproduced below:

Husband's social class
I & II 0.7
III 0.8
IV 1.1
V 1.9
Other 1.6
No husband 2.3

Mother's age	*Birth order*	
Less than 20	1st	1.3
	2nd	2.9
	3rd+	7.0
20–24	1st	0.8
	2nd	1.3
	3rd	1.8
	4th+	3.0
25–29	1st	0.3
	2nd	0.6
	3rd	1.0
	4th+	1.4
30 plus	1st	0.2
	2nd	0.4
	3rd	0.6
	4th+	0.9

Interval from last pregnancy to this conception
Less than 6 months 2.0
6 months or more 0.8
No previous pregnancy 1.0

Date of last monthly period
Known by mother 0.9
Not known 1.9

Smoked during pregnancy
None 0.6
1–19 per day 1.3
20 or more 2.6

Infection during pregnancy
Yes 2.0
No 0.9

Maternal Drug Addiction
Yes 5.0

Mother took Barbiturates
Yes 2.5

Month of delivery
March–June 0.8
July 0.9
Aug–Dec 1.2
Jan–Feb 1.0

Sex of infant
Boy 1.1
Girl 0.9

Gestation
Less than 35 weeks 3.9
36 weeks 2.1
37 weeks plus 0.9

Birthweight
Less than 2,500g 1.9
2,500–2,999g 1.2
3,000g plus 0.8

Multiple births
Singleton 1.0
Twin 2.7
Triplet 5.7

Congenital defect present
Yes 2.0

Previous sudden infant death
Yes 3.0

The individual scores in the above system should be *multiplied* together to give the final relative risks score. Quoting the two examples used in *Sudden Infant Death: Patterns, Puzzles and Problems*, Golding *et al*, may help to show how the scoring system should be used and how the results may be interpreted.

In Example A, Mr and Mrs Jones are of social class III (he is a car mechanic), and are both in their early twenties. This was their first baby. The pregnancy had been uneventful, apart from a bout of flu in the first month. Mrs Jones smoked about fifteen cigarettes a day. Their baby boy was delivered in August after a gestation of thirty-six weeks. He weighed 2,650g. The scores to be multiplied together are as follows:

0.8 (social class III)
0.8 (first baby to mother aged 20–24)
2.0 (infection in pregnancy)
1.3 (mother smoked 1–19 cigarettes a day)
1.1 (boy)
2.1 (gestation thirty-six weeks)
1.2 (birthweight 2,500–2,999g)

Multiplying these scores together gives a composite score of 4.6. This implies that baby Jones is four times more susceptible to the risk of sudden infant death than other babies in the population.

In Example B, Jane Gordon's fiancé was killed in a car crash during the early part of her pregnancy. She was 28 years old when she gave birth to this her third child. She had never smoked. There was a gap of four years between this and her previous children. She was not sure of the date of her last menstrual period and she gave birth to a girl weighing 3,250g in March. The scores to be multiplied together are as follows:

2.3 (no husband)
1.0 (aged 25–29, third baby)
0.8 (six months plus since last pregnancy)
0.6 (non-smoker)
1.9 (date of LMP not known)
0.9 (girl)
0.8 (birthweight 3,000 plus)
0.8 (March birth)

Multiplying these scores together gives a composite score of 1.2. Thus baby Gordon's risk of sudden infant death is only slightly above the average.

Even where the baby's score is high, the actual risk of a cot death remains very small indeed. The following table shows the daily risk of a particular child dying suddenly and unexpectedly at each age in a population with an incidence of 2.5 cot deaths per 1,000 live births:

Age of child	Risk of death
Less than 4 weeks	1 in 164,800
4–7 weeks	1 in 82,400
8–11 weeks	1 in 57,680
12–15 weeks	1 in 74,425
16–19 weeks	1 in 135,700
20–23 weeks	1 in 209,750
24–39 weeks	1 in 314,600
40 weeks plus	1 in 470,000

In the case of baby Jones, his risk would be calculated by dividing the figures on the right of the above table by 4.6. Thus the risk in his first four weeks of life would be 1 in 35,826 per day, and for the next four weeks they would be 1 in 17,913 – in other words, the risk would still be exceptionally small.

It only makes sense to use a scoring system if identification of babies at high risk of cot death assists in preventing cot death from happening. There is as yet no final proof that using a scoring system to identify high-risk babies acts as a preventive measure, but it is interesting to note that in some areas where extra health-visitor support has been provided for babies thought to be at 'high risk', the rate of cot death has shown a reduction. It seems possible, if the following factors do have a causative role to play, that sudden infant deaths could be reduced if:

(1) Mothers did not smoke, either during the pregnancy or after the child was born.
(2) Women delayed having children until the age of 25 or so.
(3) Coupled avoided rapid successive pregnancies by the use of reliable methods of family planning.
(4) Women avoided the use of drugs during pregnancy and breast-feeding, since these could endanger the child's health.

Medical intervention

It is very difficult to know whether minor symptoms displayed by some babies and children prior to their sudden and unexpected deaths are random or relevant. It is important, therefore, for doctors, health visitors and health carers to indicate to parents what symptoms should be taken seriously and to assure parents that medical support and help will be available if it is sought. Children within the age range of cot death need to be kept constantly under review whilst they are showing symptoms, however trivial these may seem in themselves. There are still a number of doctors who do not realize that cot deaths can happen up until the age of 2 and that they may or may not be preceded by symptoms. As a guideline for parents, the Foundation for a number of years has published suggestions about when to consult a doctor about your baby and these are reproduced in Appendix 3. It is now considering updating these suggestions in the light of new research on babies' symptoms and their significance.

In order to try and support parents coping with a subsequent baby following a cot death and also as a possible preventive measure, the Foundation has established a scheme in England known as CONI –Care of the Next Infant. Full details about this scheme are given in Chapter 8, but essentially CONI consists of a protocol for support for families from paediatricians, nurse managers, co-ordinators, health visitors and general practitioners, with weekly home visits by the health visitor, symptom diaries, regular weighing and use of weight charts and, if appropriate, measurement of environmental temperature and use of an apnoea monitor. Once established throughout the country, it is hoped that CONI may provide a valuable weapon in the fight against cot death and also raise the level of health care for babies and young children.

Care in the home

One of the effects of research into cot deaths has been a heightened awareness of the importance of good health care in the home. Without undermining parents' faith in themselves, professionals do have a duty to emphasize to new parents the need to be vigilant about hygiene and about the correct making up of feeds if the baby is bottle-fed. They also need to offer practical advice about how much clothing and wrapping to use on the baby, since both excessive heat and cold may be harmful. The modern tendency seems to be to overwrap our babies and many modern synthetic materials do not allow sweat to evaporate from the skin. Allowances for temperature changes have to be made – what is suitable for a baby who is outside in the pram may be decidedly too much once the pram is transferred to a centrally heated house. An even temperature of 66°F (19°C) is a good guide and it is worth investing in a maximum/minimum room thermometer. Babies need to be well wrapped until about 1 month of age, but thereafter you should let yourself be guided by what would feel comfortable to an adult in the way of clothing and bedding. A baby can overheat quickly and in cold weather lose heat quickly – a sensible way of checking is to remove the covers and clothing just enough to be able to feel the skin of your baby's tummy, as this will provide a much more accurate indication of true body temperature than that suggested by a baby's cheeks or hands or toes.

Physical contact and sensory stimulation

Babies need their sleep, but there is some suggestion that leaving babies unattended in separate rooms for long intervals of time may not be a good idea. In overcrowded areas of the world such as Bangladesh and Hong Kong, where prevailing risk factors would suggest that the rate of cot death could be expected to be high, the rate is surprisingly low and it is thought that in part this may be due to the fact that babies in such areas are surrounded by people and noise and are rarely left in isolation. Babies in these areas also tend to sleep in other people's arms or strapped to their backs, not on their own in a prone position in cots. If your instinct tells you to keep your baby close to you, give plenty of cuddles and allow the baby to share your bed at night, then be true to your instincts, provided always that you and your partner are sober and in control and therefore able to sense if the baby is in any discomfort or distress. As mentioned before, overlaying has already been discounted as a cause of cot death, but obviously an adult rendered almost unconscious through drink or drugs could roll on top of the baby without being aware of doing so and suffocation could result. In our own experience, it is the adults who tend to suffer, not the baby. Both Mary and later her brother Christopher shared our bed for their first two years. They slept without problem but we were sensitive to every movement and sound, to say nothing of flailing feet and elbows! Naturally such a solution would not suit every couple, but lovemaking need not suffer; losing access to one's usual bed certainly makes for ingenuity and inventiveness as far as finding comfortable but unoccupied areas of the house is concerned! If you do want the privacy of your own bed, it is worth bearing in mind that a soundly sleeping baby can often be transferred temporarily to its own cot or pram provided it is done carefully! One bonus of sharing the bed with your baby is the close physical contact which results and this can encourage your baby to become very affectionate and loving in later life.

Where cot death is concerned, we are all still learning. It is a jigsaw where there is no picture on the box lid to act as a guide. Both the shape and the size of the puzzle are unknown and some of the pieces in the box may prove not to belong to it at all, but progress is being made and there *is* hope for the future.

2

Coping with Grief – the Baby's Mother

Cot death is a parent's nightmare. Like many other parents throughout the world, I have learnt at a high price what happens when that nightmare becomes a reality. By sharing in this chapter how I learnt at first hand about sudden infant death and about grieving and about coping and failing to cope, I'm hoping that if you are also a bereaved mother you will be able to use my experiences and those of other cot-death families known to me to help you in coping with your own. If you are a relative, friend or professional involved in some way, I'm hoping that the chapter will enable you to gain some insights into the needs of bereaved mothers and how best to offer your support.

On 10 June 1979 I gave birth, seven weeks prematurely, to twin girls, Elizabeth and Mary. Elizabeth was born first. At 4 lbs she weighed 4 oz less than Mary but she was strong and active, whereas Mary was very weak at birth, needed oxygen and, later, phototherapy treatment for jaundice. After five very anxious weeks in the Special Care Baby Unit they were both able to come home, much to our relief and the great excitement of our 4-year-old daughter Rebecca. The weeks that followed were hectic and we found ourselves delighted by our lovely twins but exhausted with looking after them. On 5 September I went to a meeting of our local Twins Club and asked for ideas on how to get some sleep.

'Oh, don't have the twins in your bedroom, put them in one of their own,' came the advice. 'I couldn't,' I said. 'I'd be too worried about cot death' – so yes, I'd heard of it, but how naive to assume that it could only happen in cots and only happen at night.

The following morning I bathed and dressed Elizabeth, breastfed her while reading a story to Rebecca and then, because the sun was shining, laid Elizabeth in the twin pram and wheeled her out into the garden. Mary was still soundly asleep in her carrycot upstairs. Just after checking on Elizabeth, by now also sound asleep, the phone rang – a mother I had met recently with twins of her own, asking to come round and meet mine. I hastily tidied, she arrived, we chatted for a while and then Mary began to cry. I went up to her in the bedroom, changed her, brought her downstairs and tried to feed her, but she refused and continued to cry, so I took her out to the pram to check on Elizabeth and in the hope that wheeling Mary back and forwards for a while would settle her.

Elizabeth was lying face downwards. She had wriggled off the end of the foam mattress, pushing it beneath her and forcing her head against the end of the interior. I laid Mary down and picked up Elizabeth, feeling wetness gush out of her as I did so. 'She's been sick,' I thought, and then saw that there was some blood in the vomit. I turned her over. One of her cheeks was white, the other purplish-blue and mottled, her face somehow flat and distorted. I can remember saying rapidly: 'Oh my God, oh my God,' over and over, almost like a litany. I think I knew that she was dead but ludicrously I began to pump her arm up and down as if by rousing her in such a way I could inflate life back into her. Then reason returned and I ran with her into the house, my first thoughts for Rebecca. I didn't want her to see this baby whose colour was so wrong. I sat on the stairs cradling Elizabeth and called to my friend to leave Rebecca in the lounge and telephone for an ambulance. Then I remembered another friend – Margaret, a midwife, living opposite. I ran, Elizabeth hugged against my shoulder, my sandals clattering stupidly on the road. Training tells. Within seconds Elizabeth was on Margaret's hall carpet and Margaret was massaging her heart. Then the mouth-to-mouth resuscitation began, while I stood silently pleading with God, promising anything if only Elizabeth could be allowed to come back to me. At one point she raised her arm and I thought she'd revived. I realize now that it was probably just a reflex action. I wonder if it was in that moment that her spirit left her. I prefer to think so, leaving me in the full knowledge of my love, not dying out in the garden in such total isolation.

Two ambulancemen arrived and applied oxygen. The doctor I'd somehow telephoned also arrived and directed how much oxygen to give. By now I did know, even before he told them, that it was useless to continue. Even then I was still me, right up to the moment when the ambulanceman looked up and I saw that he was fighting back tears. It was the shock of realizing that other people could feel grief as well that proved too much. I'd been crying to myself, but I didn't cry any louder; I just simply left my own body. I wanted to go with Elizabeth, so the essential 'me' that I know, left and went to hover in a corner, looking at Elizabeth's body on the couch and watching the colour drain from her, while the purely mechanical me refused the doctor's offer of tranquillizers and later answered the questions of the coroner's officer who arrived, clipboard in hand.

Before the ambulancemen left, I was allowed to hold Elizabeth again and briefly she seemed real, but once back on the couch her body became merely a shell, like a cocoon after the butterfly has flown.

I stayed outside myself too long, I think, because I sometimes feel as if the two parts of me have never properly fused again. What brought me briefly back to myself was the arrival of my husband Pat, but his pain and his grief were so profound that I could not help him and off I went again, separating from myself with distinct relief. Someone brought Mary to me for feeding and I sat on a chair, feeding the baby who was alive and with me and looking at the body of the baby who had died and was gone. It was the mechanical part, the play-acting part, that told Rebecca that her sister was dead. The intensity of her anger frightened me. '*Why? Why* did she die?' she demanded over and over again, echoing my own bewilderment and starting us unknowingly on to the long road of grief.

Cot death in young babies and in older children

When a baby dies, we have very little past together. What we lose is the entire future which we would have shared. A baby's death goes completely against hope and against expectation and that is why it is so devastating and so crushing. The suddenness and the un-expectedness both add to the trauma, because there is no warning when a cot death happens and therefore no time to prepare. Many of these deaths take place at around 3 months and emotionally this is a critical time. As experts have pointed out, mothers are still making post-natal and hormonal adjustments at that stage and are coping with all the exhaustion caused by motherhood and night feeds. It is a time when parents are forming deep bonds with their baby, only to have these bonds shattered by an event for which no one can offer an explanation.

There is no 'easy' time to lose a child. The grief is profound no matter what the age at the time, but there are marked differences in the experiences felt by those who have lost a young baby and those who have lost an older child through cot death. When the baby has very little past, that past becomes very precious indeed. I regret deeply the photos I never took, the moments I never captured, those many other moments which I wasted on household chores and trivia and which I could have spent with Elizabeth if only I'd known how little time we were going to have together. This holds true for all cot-death parents but try not to let it become a stick with which to beat yourself.

When an older child dies, there are more memories and these can be very painful, but in time they can become valued and bring comfort. Jill, whose son Duncan died at the age of 1½ years, told me that she did not regret the memories at all, that she would willingly go through it all again to have the time with him again. She told me of her clearest memory – how Duncan would sit in his babyseat behind her in the car, how she would smile at him in her rear-view mirror and how much, after his death, she missed his smiley face beaming back at her, to the extent that, for a while, she could still see him.

With a young baby, we are left wondering how his or her personality would have developed. With an older child, there has been more time to discover that personality and to watch it blossom. Either way, the loss is immense.

Mothers of older children who die suddenly are a long way from pregnancy and they have no expectation of death at all because their child is through the danger period of being young and vulnerable. Having gone through all the hard work involved in looking after a baby and having watched a delightful child emerge from the chaos of night feeds and nappies and seemingly endless crying sessions, it can be very difficult indeed to contemplate having to go back and start all over again, especially if they had assumed that their families were now complete.

Mothers of young babies who die suddenly usually have to face quite different problems. In many cases they will have been breastfeeding and have to cope with the stark and painful reality of a plentiful supply of milk and no baby to whom it can be given. How to ease this problem from a practical point of view is explained in Chapter 6. How to ease it from an emotional point of view is not so straightforward and the craving to feed and cradle the absent baby can be very strong indeed.

Young babies are very dependent on their parents and can expect attention for what often seems like twenty-four hours a day. When the baby suddenly and unexpectedly dies, the parents can feel totally lost because, having been so busy, they are abruptly no longer needed. The physical routine all at once ceases and the emotional pattern of their lives is completely shattered.

Each stage of a child's life has its own special joys and therefore its own special pains when the child dies. Parents who lose a toddler suddenly find that they do not know what to do with their hands when out walking because there is no pushchair to push and no small hand to hold in theirs. 'I just didn't know how to walk down the road on my own.' When parents are used to chattering away to their toddler all day and having 'help' with all the household activities, the silence and absence following the toddler's death is like a chasm from which there is no escape, since every room and every household item and toy holds a memory. Sometimes these parents receive less help and understanding than parents whose babies die when they are very young. Cot death over the age of 1 year is very rare and consequently people tend not to know that it can happen. Because they find it so difficult to believe and are so deeply embarrassed by it, they tend to keep away from the families concerned instead of offering the support which is so greatly needed. As cot-death parents, it is difficult enough for us to believe and accept what has happened to our baby even if our baby has died during the 'peak' time. For parents who lose a toddler it is more difficult. In addition to the appalling irony that their child has survived babyhood only to succumb after becoming an apparently healthy youngster, they have to cope with the reality that they are the bad news that no one wants to hear – that on very rare occasions older children can and do die in cot deaths. In 1987 in England and Wales there were forty-six such deaths. The fact that this is so rare may be of comfort to other parents but not to the families concerned. Everyone associates cot death with babies and this can make families who lose an older child feel very hurt that their toddlers are being somehow excluded. Each time they meet new parents anxiously counting the months until their baby can pass the 'danger' time, they know that being asked to give their own child's age at death will cause shock, distress and a rise in anxiety level. They also know that if ever they have a subsequent baby, for them the waiting time for a 'safe' age will be very long indeed.

Time seems to be the enemy at whatever age the baby dies. Parents whose baby dies at a young age are denied time, denied the chance to get to know their baby well and to watch him or her develop and grow. The craving to be allowed time back with our baby or toddler is sometimes overwhelming. Cot death is so sudden and so very, very final.

Grief reactions

At the time of Elizabeth's death, I assumed that our reactions were unique to us. In a way they were, for we are all individuals and there are no right or wrong reactions, only natural ones, but what has surprised me in looking back is the recognition of how clearly we have moved through each stage. These stages were outlined for me when I attended a Study Day on cot deaths at Bristol in May 1982 and heard Dr Richard Williams, a consultant child psychiatrist, give a very helpful talk on the effects of cot death. He divided the grieving into four main stages: firstly, numbing; secondly, disbelief; thirdly, disorganization and fourthly, reorganization, which can take years to achieve. I soon learnt that there are no short-cuts to grief but that there are certain milestones, and I can still remember awarding myself mental 'ticks' each time a situation was faced and overcome. One mistake I made was to assume that grief, because it has a definite beginning, must also have a definite end, that there would come a time when I could say: 'There, we're through it and it's over.' I know now that grief has no end. We can learn to reorganize and to adjust our lives but it seems likely that the grief, though it alters as we alter, will always remain part of us.

Numbing and shock

As far as the first stage of numbing is concerned, the shock is almost a help because it acts as an anaesthetic. It is when the initial shock wears off that the real, physical pain begins. I can understand now how people can die of a broken heart, because the pain in my chest was so severe that even breathing was difficult, and so intense in my head that I felt that something would have to burst to relieve the pressure. As a cot-death parent you may well be offered tranquillizers by your doctor. Whilst it may be tempting to accept, these only postpone the pain, they don't remove it. If you feel that prolonging the period of numbness may help, then by all means accept the use of tranquillizers, but you will have to accept, too, that sooner or later the reality of your baby's death has to be faced and grieving allowed to begin. The use of alcohol may also deaden the pain for a while but, again, this is only a temporary effect and not a long-term solution. As someone once neatly put it: 'I drank to drown my sorrows, but they soon all learnt how to swim.'

Because we are all individuals we all respond differently to the shock of our baby's sudden death. Some parents may feel a strong need to have company, the physical comfort and reassurance of others around them, while others may need to shut themselves away until the shock subsides. Some may feel the need to make themselves busy, notifying relatives and friends and making funeral arrangements, but others may cope best with the shock if they can be treated like a child for a while and tucked into bed with a warm drink and maybe even a hot water bottle to cuddle for support. It helps greatly if other people can be sensitive to the differing needs of parents immediately after the baby's death, for offering the right sort of help at that time can do much to reduce the trauma and aid recovery.

In a survey carried out by Lady Limerick of 713 questionnaires concerning sudden infant deaths in England during the two periods of 1974–79 and 1980–81, 86 per cent of the deaths happened in the home, 5.5 per cent in a car and 5 per cent in a public place. Only 3 per cent occurred on the way to hospital or within twenty-four hours of admission. The immediate reaction of those finding the baby varied: some could only scream for help, others tried resuscitation. Some rang their GP and/or an ambulance, others ran to a neighbour for help or drove their baby to the nearest place of help – surgery, health centre, hospital or even police station. In 68 per cent of the survey, an ambulance was called and the majority of parents found the ambulance staff kind and efficient. In 54 per cent the death was confirmed at a hospital rather than by a GP and in 78 per cent of those cases, at least one parent went to the hospital.

Few outsiders can appreciate the enormity of the shock felt by cot-death families. No one who has found a baby suddenly and unexpectedly dead ever forgets that experience, it scars for life. When the memory is fresh it is very harrowing indeed, yet one way in which the mind tries to accept and come to terms with it seems to be by insisting on going over and over it all, replaying it like an obscene video until the shock subsides. When I tried to block out the memory of Elizabeth's discoloured face the image simply returned in nightmares until I allowed myself to acknowledge and think about her. Gradually, very gradually, the image faded until the day came when I could see her again as she had been in life, not in death, but it does take time, so it helps if you can be aware that nightmares are likely to recur for a while – they will eventually cease.

Disbelief

When Elizabeth died it seemed incredible to me that the world could carry on so normally. Buses were still moving, people were still out walking and shopping – didn't they know? How could the outside world be so unaffected when our own small world had been so completely devastated? I felt very clearly at the time that the day of Elizabeth's death was a tape which I should have been allowed to erase and re-run so that I could do it all differently. Healthy babies don't just die, so I knew that there must have been something wrong which I'd failed to notice. I was therefore to blame, but it was only a first offence; I felt I should have been allowed off with a caution, not exposed to the full rigour of some unknown law. It was too final. I could cope with losing her for a week, a month, even years, but not for the rest of my life. I was being asked to accept the unacceptable –that our lovely and apparently healthy daughter could simply cease living and, having done so, could never come back to us.

Feelings of madness

Even though as a cot-death mother you know that your baby is dead, it is impossible to believe it, so be patient with yourself. Wanting to feed and cuddle your baby so much that you ache all over is perfectly normal. Imagining that you can hear your dead baby cry is perfectly normal. Searching for the baby that you know already is no longer there, this too is perfectly normal.

The full impact of Elizabeth's death hit me the following day. I came out of our dining-room and saw the empty pram in the hall. It was the finality of her going that made the pain unendurable, so that I found myself beating my head against the adjoining wall, beating to make something explode and release me. That moment of total despair and insanity probably saved me. I came back to reality, looked at the wall which friends had helped us to paint and wondered how many ghosts I had just installed into it. I've learnt since that a feeling of impending madness is a natural part of the grieving process, that far from being in danger of losing our reason, we are simply responding to what has happened to us. If so, I was a model pupil, conforming to all the right patterns, for after the momentary madness came the long, tangible depression and despair.

Feelings of despair

Everything that had once seemed important, now seemed irrelevant. All the everyday workings and concerns of our lives were just so much trivia. 'Vanity, vanity, all is vanity.' What on earth was it all for? Cooking meals, watching television, choosing what to wear – all futile, all a waste of time. Getting up out of a chair became a physical feat requiring considerable effort. I'd read of people lying down in the snow to die. The snow of despair enveloping me might not have been cold but it was certainly no less real and the temptation to lie down and not get up again was very real, too.

I can well understand why some parents consider suicide when their baby dies, even though it is not the solution and only adds to the pain felt by everyone who has any connection with the family. For me it was never an option because I felt that it would separate me from Elizabeth not just for life but for eternity and what I wanted more than anything was to be reunited with her. Nor did I feel that I would need to actively take my own life, because it seemed to me impossible that I could continue living. I'd heard that the bodies of beheaded chickens could afterwards run around for a while on a purely reflex basis. I felt the same. Elizabeth's death had split my soul from my body and, though my body was continuing to function, I felt that it could only be a matter of time before I could cease to be and could go and join her again. By the time I had realized that this was not going to happen and that I was going to continue living whether I wanted to do so or not, the feelings connected with suicide had passed. My love was as great as ever for my husband Pat, for our older daughter Rebecca and for Elizabeth's surviving twin Mary, but I was so far away – it wasn't love that made me continue looking after them, it was a simple mechanical response, doing my duty as wife and mother.

Feelings of anger

I read somewhere that depression is anger turned inwards upon itself. In that case, I must have been very angry indeed. I'm sure I was. It showed itself outwardly in brief flashes of fury over trivial frustrations, fury which would erupt and then subside as quickly as it had come. With some parents, this anger may direct itself outwards towards the doctor, health visitor or anyone in recent contact with the baby, or it may direct itself towards other parents with a small baby of their own. These may be friends or even total strangers and there can be a sense of true rage that they are being allowed the privilege of still having their baby when, despite all the love that we had to give, our own much-loved baby has died. For believers there may well be a feeling of intense anger towards God, either for taking the baby or at the very least for standing by and allowing the death to happen. There may even be feelings of anger towards the dead baby for leaving, a sense that if our baby had truly loved us, he or she would not have died and caused us such pain. Although this is totally irrational, since our babies do not choose to die in such a way, nevertheless the sense of rejection can be very real and the accompanying anger must be faced and recognized if it is to be overcome.

Feelings of fear

Elizabeth's death removed all sense of security and all guarantees. She had seemed healthy and normal and she had died, so where did that leave the rest of us? Mary, her twin, was most at risk and I did not dare to let her out of my sight. During the day she moved around the house with me, in a baby carrier or in her baby bouncer, or else she slept in her cot in the lounge while I watched near by. At night she slept in our bed. I knew that Pat's arm moved to check on her breathing just as often as mine did. What I did not know until months later was that, during my short spells of sleep, his arm also checked me as often as mine checked him during his own brief rests. We both used to go into Rebecca's room during the night, holding our own breaths until we could be certain of hearing hers. On the occasions when she asked if she or Mary would die as well, we reassured her with a confidence which I know we did not feel and which I suspect she could sense, only too well.

Disorganization

The third recognized stage of grieving, that of disorganization, creates practical problems for any mother trying to look after her family and home, especially if she is also working. Memory and concentration are both severely affected and great tolerance and understanding is needed by partners, friends and colleagues. A cot death not only removes security, it also destroys self-confidence. I had been responsible for Elizabeth's safety and well-being and she had died while in my care. Whichever way I looked at it, I had failed her, so guilt loomed large and this, combined with the loss of self-confidence, contributed greatly to the sense of disorganization.

Much of my daily routine could be done on auto-pilot, but because my internal disorganization was so severe, trivial happenings could defeat me easily and frequently did so. I can clearly remember standing in a supermarket fighting back tears of frustration because I couldn't decide between two different brands of soup. We didn't even need any soup! When I was safely at home, minor irritations and difficulties could produce major onsets of tears, and I stayed bright and breezy in company only to dissolve hopelessly once the front door was firmly closed. With hindsight I realize that it would have been better to show and share some of my pain instead of trying to lock it all inside and pretend that everything was normal, so if you are given the chance to express your grief, take every opportunity to do so and don't try to 'put on a brave face' all the time – the cost is too high.

If you find it too difficult to express yourself openly to others, it is worth considering the suggestion made in Chapter 4 concerning the way children cope with grief – namely to express your feelings through writing, drawing or painting. A year after Elizabeth died I wrote the following poem about her and it helped me to cope with what I was feeling at the time.

Elizabeth

I thought I could swim but I find I can barely tread water.
I relive that morning – no warning, so well and so real:
I bathed you and dressed you and fed you, no danger in daytime –
The thought of you gnaws at a rawness that time does not heal.

At lunchtime, your pram in the sunshine, the radio talking,
I went out to check you and saw you were sleeping, content.
The phone went – a friend: could she visit? I hastily tidied,
She came and we chattered and frittered the half-hour we spent.

The binmen came, clattering lids, and I went out to check you –
Dead . . . you were dead . . . you were dead, oh dear God, you were dead.
How could our cord have been cut with no slice of the knifeblade?
Life doesn't end at three months when your whole life's ahead.

You died so alone yet so near and it buffets like breakers.
I should have been with you, it drags at me, tugging me down.
I'm only afloat with the rafters of friends and my family –
It's hard to stay surfaced when part of you's wanting to drown.

The binmen are clattering lids and the radio's talking.
Thursday, the day that you died, and a year has gone by.
Groundless, I'm floundering, wounded yet walking – in water
That thwarts with the not-knowing-how and the not-knowing-why.

Acceptance will come, there's so much that we can't understand.
In the grief of this world what's the measure of one baby daughter?
I still have belief; the sea's calmer; I know I'll reach land,
But I thought I could swim and I find I can barely tread water.

Reorganization

The fourth stage, reorganization, is a long, slow process. From my own experience and from talking to other mothers whose babies have died suddenly and inexplicably, the single most crucial piece of advice which I would offer is this: allow yourself to grieve. Don't try to shut away the pain because it won't be shut away. Emotion denied now will simply resurface later in life, possibly in a more damaging form. Thankfully, whereas society still expects fathers to be 'strong' and to conceal their pain, an unfair and harmful expectation, mothers at least are sometimes allowed to talk about what has happened. Use this, talk about your baby and about yourself as much as you can. Don't worry that you may be boring your relatives and friends or embarrassing them with the rawness of your emotions. They, too, need to grieve for the loss of your baby, their lives, too, are touched deeply by your tragedy, so tell your family and friends of your needs and share the grief. Emotion *is* embarrassing, but sharing it can bring tremendous relief to all concerned. Friends can feel very helpless at such a time and are likely to avoid using your baby's name or talking about your baby's death for fear of distressing you – but since you are already so deeply distressed, speak about it and give them the opportunity to help, instead of feeling excluded and inadequate.

Because I felt so vulnerable, I grew a form of protective armour around myself, staying permanently steeled and tense in order to avoid the risk of being caught 'offguard', such as when I summoned up courage to take Mary for her clinic check-up three weeks after

Elizabeth's death and the health visitor in charge of the weighing said: 'Oh, it's one of the twins, how lovely – where's the other one?' Protective armour was essential in the early months, but of course it served to keep out those wanting to help just as much as those unintentionally causing harm. It was then that I began to award myself 'ticks' for progress. The first time that I could force myself to look into someone else's pram without my stomach lurching over in anticipation of the dead baby I would find . . . the first time that I could hold someone else's baby and manage to suppress the overwhelming fear that my Jonah touch would cause its death as well . . . coping with the first Christmas . . . with Mary's first birthday, a celebration for everyone but also a deep mourning . . . the first anniversary of Elizabeth's death, which for outsiders was simply an ordinary day . . . gradually dates were faced and passed, life took on some semblance of normality; I found that I could laugh at jokes again without feeling somehow guilty. It may help to know that, having talked to other bereaved mothers, I have found that these feelings which I had assumed were peculiar to me are in fact very common and that the situations which we dread most can be faced and can be overcome.

Recovery

As a child, whenever something distressing happened to me my mother would say: 'Never mind, dear, it's character-forming.' Thanks, but given the choice I'd have preferred less pain and less character. Cot-death parents are not given the choice, but if we can allow ourselves to grieve openly and fully, recovery can take place. At the time it seems difficult to believe that recovery of any kind is possible, the shock and the grief are so overwhelming that to imagine life ever being 'normal' again seems impossible, but it honestly does come. We are not the same people as we were before our babies died. Part of us dies with our baby and there is no point in trying to pretend otherwise. In mourning the loss of our child we mourn also the loss of the person we once were, but we need not be left emotionally and spiritually handicapped. A new person does form out of the depth of the pain, not the same and not the person we would have chosen to be. I cannot imagine anyone willingly opting for such pain, but when it is imposed on us by a cot death, the learning experience truly can become the most profound and most valuable ever to happen to us.

Nothing compensates for a baby's death and nothing justifies it. Being told that good can come from it, that we may become better, more understanding and more sympathetic people because of it is no consolation. Nevertheless, it is true. Coping with the devastating effects of a cot death equips us well for coping with other life experiences and for gaining insight into the needs and problems of those around us.

You will be told repeatedly by well-meaning people that: 'Time is a great healer.' When I had to endure this I wanted to cry out: 'But I don't want to be healed, I want my baby back and if I can't have her I'll have this pain instead; it's all I have left of her and at least it's mine.' Such a feeling was right and normal at the time, but I'm glad now that I didn't allow it to rule my life forever or trap me in an emotional prison, and I'm grateful for the degree of emotional growth which has since been allowed to take place. Don't try to deny or minimize your grief, but on the other hand, try not to let it shackle your life. Work through it, be kind to yourself, be patient with yourself and realistic in your expectations and you will find that in time you are able to live again and not just to exist. After a cot death nothing is ever taken for granted again and priorities become very clear. Because there are no certainties any more, the focus is taken away from a future which may never happen and is placed instead on today, so that each day tends to be enjoyed for its own sake. Although it might not seem imaginable at the time, happiness does become possible again and as cot-death parents we are able to recognize and appreciate it all the more because of the intensity of the pain out of which it has been born.

Coping as a single parent

When cot death strikes those coping as single parents, they have the added strain of having no partner at home to shoulder some of the burden or offer comfort and support. If they already have older children or the responsibility of a job, then they have no opportunity to let go for a while, for these responsibilities will continue, with no one to ease the pressures for them. If they do not have a job and it is their only baby or child who has died, then they can feel very aimless indeed and will find waking and getting up in the mornings increasingly difficult unless they can find a valid reason for doing so.

On occasions it may be the father who was coping as the single parent prior to his baby's death (if the relationship has failed and the mother has decided to leave both partner and child or sadly, if the mother has died during or after birth or been admitted to hospital for post-natal depression or other illness). More frequently it is the mother who was caring for her baby prior to death. Either way, the awareness of having had total responsibility for the baby's welfare can increase the sense of guilt when the baby dies suddenly and unexpectedly, even though the death could not have been predicted or prevented.

If the baby was the outcome of a relationship which has later failed, then the baby's subsequent death can seem like the final blow, proof that a once loving relationship has died in every sense and therefore an additional grief to bear.

It could be argued that at least single parents can focus on their own needs during bereavement, without having to cope with the strain of trying to answer their partners' needs as well. They are free to express their grief when and how they wish, without fear of distressing or angering anyone else in the house, but this is of poor comfort to anyone needing love and support. With any cot-death parent there is always a tendency to feel lonely and isolated, no matter how many friends and relatives live near by. With a single parent this is even more the case and it can add to the sense of aimlessness and the risk of feeling: 'What's the point in living?' Single parents, therefore, should try and seek help from as many sources as they need (potential sources are listed in Chapter 7) and it is worth remembering that the calm and compassionate volunteers of the Samaritans organization are always available during moments of despair. The greater the need for help, the more difficult it can be to seek it and those connected in any way with bereaved single parents should be aware of this and try and ensure that they are never left in isolation with their grief.

Financial problems are likely to be greater for single parents because they are more likely than married couples to be trying to cope on Income Support. In addition to all the other stresses, therefore, they may have to face the extra strain of coping with officialdom to try and obtain financial help for the funeral expenses. If this is so, then the presence of a friend or relative can be of great help and support, giving company while queuing and acting as spokesperson if the bereaved parent finds the ordeal too great.

After a cot death we all need at some point to pick up the pieces of our shattered lives and try to make a fresh start with what remains to us. For single parents this is especially difficult. Already damaged in confidence by whatever has caused them to become single parents in the first place, their self-confidence and self-esteem are further destroyed by the baby's death and the time when they most need to go out, meet people and perhaps apply for a job, is the time when they will feel least able to do so. Again, relatives and friends can do much to restore self-esteem and self-confidence and should do all they can to help. They also have a vital role to play if a mother or father becomes a single parent after a subsequent baby is born. Not all marriages survive the strain of a cot death, so parents who had the support of a partner when their previous baby died may find themselves having to cope as a single parent during the pregnancy or after the birth of a subsequent child. The problems which tend to be experienced when caring for the next child (which are mentioned in Chapter 8) tend to be greater when coping alone, so it helps if friends and family can give all they can in the way of practical and emotional support.

Coping as a couple

A cot death threatens to destroy the very essence of our respective roles as parents. Traditionally the mother is the one who feeds and baths and dresses and looks after the baby, who has the most intimate physical relationship with the baby at a young age and who, through her caring, fulfils her nurturing role. Traditionally, too, the father is the protector and provider, the one who finds the money for the rent or mortgage and who does all he can to maintain his home and safeguard his family from danger or distress. Through his actions he fulfils his protective and providing role. When the baby suddenly dies, both these parental roles may appear to have died as well, leaving the parents aimless and helpless. For fathers used to action, going out to work to earn the money to provide for the needs of their family, this sense of helplessness can be very damaging and difficult to handle. 'I felt I'd failed my baby, that I should have been able to save him. But I wasn't even there when he died, I was at work. When I got home there was nothing for me to do, he was already dead. I felt cheated, I felt as if I should have been able to do something to save him and I wasn't given the chance. It was so final and so unfair.'

The feeling that there *must* be something we can do to bring our babies back to life is very strong indeed, because the alternative means that our baby is totally, finally and irretrievably dead and can never return.

If both parents are there when their baby's death is discovered, it at least means that they can immediately try to comfort each other and will probably be expected to do so, but that can be very difficult when both are in a state of total shock and disbelief. On the other hand, being absent when the baby is discovered is no easier, for then there is a real risk that the parent who was not there will feel excluded from what has happened, which can make the situation seem even more unreal and difficult to accept. Reproduced below is a graph showing the time of day at which 355 cot-death babies were found dead. As can be seen from Fig. 4, as many babies died during the daytime as during the night. Of the total 43 per cent died between midnight and first being seen in the morning, 51 per cent died during the period between first being seen in the morning and 9 p.m. in the evening and 6 per cent died between 9 p.m. and midnight.

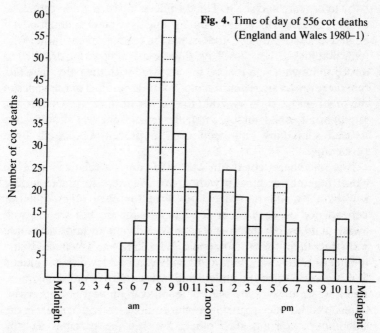

Fig. 4. Time of day of 556 cot deaths (England and Wales 1980–1)

The graph was published in the FSID Newsletter no. 25, May 1984, and was the result of Lady Limerick's survey of 713 questionnaires completed by parents during the years 1974–81.

In our case, my husband Pat was at work when I found Elizabeth dead in her pram. I would not have wished that discovery on to anyone and yet in some ways I feel that it must have been even worse for Pat. I had the closeness, for she had only just died, but for Pat it was a case of an urgent telephone call telling him that one of the twins was very ill and asking him to come home immediately, followed by a nightmarish drive trying to outrun what had already happened. I'm very grateful that Elizabeth had only just died and that my neighbour was at least able to try and revive her, even though she was unsuccessful. For over 40 per cent of parents, their baby dies during the night and is found cold and lifeless the next morning. Such parents are faced with an appalling finality and must feel battered by the unanswerable question: 'How could this happen so many hours ago without our sensing that anything was wrong?'

When Pat arrived all I could say was: 'I'm sorry, I'm so sorry,' because I felt that I had failed him so badly. He had entrusted our baby to my care and she had died while in my care. I don't think he ever blamed me for her death but I would have quite understood it if he had done so and I can understand the feelings of any father who feels that his partner must have done something wrong or failed to notice some vital sign that all was not well with the baby. The fact that there *are* no signs beforehand is of little comfort or relevance at the time; gut reaction says that the person in charge (be it partner, grandparent, child minder, neighbour or whoever) should have noticed something and been able to prevent the death from happening.

It is said that a cot death will either draw a relationship even closer together or blow it wide apart. We were fortunate in that Elizabeth's death reinforced our love for each other and our dependence on each other for mutual support, but we are well aware that how cot-death parents cope individually and as a couple will affect them for years to come. Balancing one's own needs and the needs of one's partner and family can be very difficult indeed and much tolerance and understanding is required by all concerned. The key, as always, seems to be good communication, otherwise unresolved hurts can quickly mount so that, instead of sharing the loss and comforting each other, the grieving parents can find themselves becoming more and more isolated and separated from each other.

We all grieve in our own individual ways and no two people will respond alike. The partner who needs to go out and mix with people for reassurance may seem very callous to the partner who needs to stay at home nursing the pain in private. Being honest with each other will help, but there are no easy answers, especially where one partner feels an overwhelming need to talk about the baby who has died while the other partner cannot even bear to hear the baby's name being mentioned.

Lovemaking often suffers after a cot death, yet it can be the most comforting act of all. For those brave enough to come together in the new rawness of their grief, it can provide the deepest of bonds, linking the couple in a very profound awareness of sharing and consoling. For some, though, the shock and grief can lead to a complete temporary loss of libido. Somewhere at the back of the newly bereaved mother's mind may be the thought that lovemaking can lead to pregnancy, which can lead to birth, which can lead to death. Having just been hurt so deeply by her loss, no wonder she does not want to risk being hurt in a similar way for a while. On the other hand, the craving to hold her missing baby again may make her want another baby as soon as possible, so that she may find herself wanting to make love as a means to an end, not an end in itself. Such problems can place a great strain on a partnership and, again, understanding by both partners is needed if hurts and misunderstandings are to be avoided.

What of the newly bereaved father? He may be longing for another baby to love as soon as possible but on the other hand he may genuinely feel that he cannot face going through such trauma again. Whilst lovemaking may provide a vital physical release for his pent-up emotions, unless he can explain this need to his partner she may resent him and feel: 'How can he possibly think about such an act at a time like this?' It is important for couples to try and talk both about their fears and about their needs so that they are able to help each other as much as possible.

After a cot death, parents can never be the same again and therefore their relationship as a couple will never be quite the same again. They have gained knowledge they were not seeking, at a very high price, but just as parents can grow as individuals because of the experience they have undergone and the knowledge they have gained, so they can grow as a couple and, with understanding and tolerance on both sides, their partnership can become deeper and stronger than ever.

3

Coping with Grief –
the Baby's Father

Giving a separate chapter to the grieving of fathers is not meant to imply that such grieving is completely exclusive; much of what applies to mothers applies to fathers as well. The grief of each parent is equally valid, but their ways of coping with it do tend to vary in some respects because of their differing parental roles. What does not vary is the immensity of the pain felt when the baby dies.

Fathers grieve. Because of the historical mother-and-baby, madonna-and-child association, when a cot death occurs it is easy to fall into the trap of focusing all the attention on the bereaved mother, forgetting that the father, too, has been bereaved and that his grief is just as painful and profound. He may express it differently, or not express it at all, but it is none the less there and its depth and extent should never be underestimated. Some of the most moving letters which I have received and some of the most moving conversations which I have experienced have been from and with cot-death fathers, those same fathers who are thought by many outsiders not to suffer or grieve in the way that mothers do. What came over loud and clear to me was that these fathers, far from being less affected, are so loving and caring that they tend to place their partner's needs above their own, at a high cost to themselves. Most admitted to suppressing many of their own grief reactions in order to avoid distressing their partner and to encourage the impression of coping and being strong and supportive, no matter how deep the despair they were experiencing at the time. Most felt a great need to talk about their baby's death and about their own feelings but were often denied any opportunity to do so or were faced by well-meaning outsiders saying: 'How's your poor wife, it must be terrible for her?' instead of being asked: 'How are you?'

Fathers have an extremely difficult burden to bear. Traditionally they are supposed to be the strong partner both physically and emotionally. Despite Women's Lib, they still tend to be looked upon as the practical one who will be able to mend the fuse or repair the broken vacuum cleaner. Without warning they are faced with a situation which can't be mended or repaired. The baby they loved so much is dead and they are utterly powerless; there is nothing that they can do to bring their baby back to life. As one father so poignantly expressed it: 'I felt helpless and heartbroken' and this feeling of total helplessness can be very crippling and very hard to bear. At one blow natural instincts to protect and provide are thwarted and the feeling of being profoundly and unfairly cheated makes fathers, just as much as mothers, scream inwardly: 'Why? Why our baby? Why us?'

Experiencing a cot death and trying to cope with grief affects our behaviour but fathers may not be aware of how much they have changed unless pulled up short by their other child or children asking: 'Why don't you laugh any more?' Or saying: 'You never play now.' We used to spend hours playing fantasy games with Rebecca, but after Elizabeth died I just couldn't do it any more, as if some invisible barrier was excluding me. This can be very hard for the surviving children, adding one more stress to their already disrupted home life. For many children, their fathers are their main source of fun and a way of letting off steam through boisterous games. Suddenly it all goes wrong. Their baby brother or sister dies and their father no longer wants to play, so on top of their own grief, they have to cope with what seems to them both a physical and an emotional rejection. Of course it's tempting just to say to them: 'Go away, not now, can't you see I'm too tired/too busy.' Try instead, if you possibly can, to be honest with your children and to tell them how you are feeling. If at all possible, try to join in, even when you don't feel capable of it, because doing so can help to break the vicious cycle of depression and lethargy which can be so disabling after a cot death. Even just going out for a walk together can bring a much-needed sense of togetherness and an escape from the sadness of home, while taking your older child or children to the nearest park to watch them play can make them feel still valued and loved.

Everything's so hard to bear at the time. Seeing other people's healthy children swinging and climbing may simply reinforce the awareness of what your own baby should have been able to enjoy in the future. As one father expressed it: 'I miss him more for the things we didn't do together rather than the things we did.' Both you and your baby have been cheated out of so many special moments in life, so it's not surprising if a very deep sense of anger and loss threatens to overwhelm at times, but the more you can face such situations, the easier they become. Your other children need you more than ever at such a time and any interest you can show and any reassurance you can give to them will be greatly valued.

To help me to find out how fathers try and cope following the sudden death of their baby or child, I prepared a questionnaire. There were sixteen questions, set down simply as they occurred to me and not in any order of priority. With hindsight, I could have arranged them better, but by chance they proved to be helpful to the fathers who so kindly volunteered to receive and answer them, so I am reproducing them below in the hope that thinking privately about them may help you if you are in a similar situation, and may help others to understand something of what you are experiencing and perhaps give you an opening to share your feelings:

(1) *Did others allow you to talk about your baby and about your own feelings, or did they discourage you and change the subject?*

On the whole, work colleagues did seem willing to talk about the baby's death and allow fathers to express some of their feelings, but it seemed to depend to some extent on the age group concerned. Colleagues with young children of their own tended to avoid the subject, perhaps because of the fear that cot death might strike them, too, if they acknowledged its existence. Younger female colleagues without children wanted to know more about the syndrome; older colleagues with more experience of both life and death seemed better equipped at giving fathers the opportunity to talk if they wished to do so. Where friends or work colleagues did not give the necessary openings to talk, some fathers sought such openings elsewhere, usually via the hospital chaplain, their minister of religion or local Friends of the Foundation support group.

Chris, a postman, found a total stranger the most helpful. Not knowing that his son had just recently died, she saw him trying to do his round in an obvious state of shock and grief, invited him into her kitchen and allowed him to talk and to cry and to express himself openly about his son's death.

It is very difficult for work colleagues to know what to say or do. Perhaps Andrew's associates had the right idea. Having fallen into the trap of avoiding him on the first morning because of not knowing what to say, they then sent out for a bottle of wine at lunchtime and allowed Andrew the chance to talk and to cry and to say what he was feeling, after which it became much easier both for Andrew and for his colleagues.

(2) If you were allowed to talk, is this still the case or do others imply that you should 'be over all that by now'?

It was very encouraging to learn that although after a while other people do at times tend to forget, they do not expect fathers to do so and do still allow them to talk about their baby and about their own feelings if the need arises.

(3) Do you feel able now to describe what your feelings were at the time when your baby died? If so, please could you do so.

'Lost', 'helpless', 'disorientated', 'numb', 'empty', 'angry', 'bitter' – the feelings came pouring out. It seems that it is not the case that many fathers cannot express themselves, it is that they choose not to do so because of the importance of what they see as their role of strong provider and supporter. A number of them felt that they could not place their jobs ar risk by showing their grief at work, in case they were seen as not coping, and that they could not add to their partner's distress and vulnerability by showing their grief at home. As a result, they were left with very few openings for their grief.

(4) Who helped most at the time (for example, family, friends, work colleagues, doctor, health visitor, minister, local support group, outsiders etc.)? In what ways did they help?

One answer which I had not anticipated came from Ken, whose son James died in a sudden infant death at the age of 8 months: 'People with other young children who let us play with their kids helped a lot. It made me feel that people accepted it wasn't my fault and that I wouldn't kill their kids just by being with them. That was important.'

Chris, whose son Luke died at the age of 6 weeks, expressed a deep need to cuddle a baby and was grateful to friends with young babies who allowed him to do so. This need is obviously a powerful one.

While Andrew's 10-week-old son Peter was fighting his unsuccessful battle for life in the Special Care Unit after being found dying from the sudden infant death syndrome, Andrew carried Peter's twin brother David around with him 'like my little talisman, drawing comfort from the smell of his baby hair'.

Everyone involved in a cot death received a mention at some

point during the answers to this question. Thanks and praise went to those who had helped in a practical way, like the sister-in-law who 'acted as servant for several days' and those who had proved to be good listeners, giving their time and allowing fathers to talk. The police, the chaplain, an anaesthetist, all came in for praise in this respect, the latter because he was so straightforward about the fact that the baby concerned was dead – 'his directness helped me cope with the situation'. Those who received criticism in this section did so because of insensitivity and lack of care or interest – the doctor who 'was useless, we've since changed practices', the funeral director who objected to individual requests and who failed to prevent the fact that when the father went to view his dead son he could see the opening at the back of his head, caused by the post mortem.

(5) *Would you have welcomed more help, or did you feel that it was a private grief which you preferred to handle on your own?*

Having tried to stress throughout that we are all individuals and that there are no right or wrong responses to grief, only natural ones, nowhere was it demonstrated more clearly than in the response to this question. For some fathers, the grief was very private indeed, whilst for others there was an overwhelming need to share the grief and give expression to it as much and as often as possible.

One father, Steve, said: 'I felt it was a private grief which I wanted to handle in my own way, although I think it would have helped to have talked to someone.' Ken, too, felt that: 'Too much [help] could be as bad as none at all or very little. Grief is private and needs to be handled carefully and "nurtured" to aid the individual.' Andrew, on the other hand, said with much honesty: 'It never occurred to me that grief should be private. I hurt and I wanted everyone to know I hurt. My son mattered to me and I didn't want him forgotten.'

Every bereaved father needs to decide what is appropriate for him, but, if at all possible, he also needs to explain to his partner why he is reacting in the way he has chosen, to prevent her from feeling excluded and isolated, and he needs to be sensitive to her chosen way of grieving as well.

(6) *If you felt the intense anger which so often results from a cot death, how did you cope with it? Did you want to smash something or*

did you try and bottle the anger and pretend to outsiders that you were calm and normal? What advice would you give to other fathers in a similar position?

Here again, responses varied greatly. Some said that they did not feel angry, just helpless and lost. Others felt intense anger, usually towards God, and, for a generation of supposed non-believers, it was surprising to see how strongly God featured in the replies: 'I felt very angry at God and religion. It says in the Bible God loves children but I loved him more . . . I will enter churches etc. but I cannot sit and listen to them prattle on . . .'

'My faith helped.'

'We didn't deserve this misery. Why had God allowed it to happen? . . . I began to go to church – partly to have time with my son, who was buried in the churchyard, but also to draw strength from the faith of others. Things became easier over time and, as they did, a new image of God began to form in my mind. Christ had not abandoned us but had been beside us crying.'

(7) *Did you feel that you were expected to be the strong one, supporting your partner? If so, did you welcome the role as something positive to do, or did you feel that you missed out on expressing your own feelings as a result?*

Almost without exception, the fathers who answered the questionnaire said that they were expected to be the strong one. Most welcomed the role in some way, as being something positive to do, but most also felt that as a result they had missed out on expressing their own feelings. In some cases those suppressed feelings led to anger, shouting at the very partner they were trying to support and protect. The best balance seemed to be when partners were able to be sensitive to each other's varying moods, taking it in turns to be the one supported or the one offering support, depending on individual needs at the particular time: 'We each had time to grieve and time to give comfort. Our grief brought us closer together when it could so easily have pushed us apart.'

One father commented: 'I've seen too many cases of "strong" men who are perceived by their partners as uncaring' and another astutely pointed out: 'Don't be too strong. Your wife will need help and your being "above the grief" won't help her.'

(8) *Were you allowed time off work and if so, did this help or did you*

find it easier to be at work and keeping yourself occupied?

Most fathers were allowed some time off work and needed the time at home. On returning to work, most found that it helped to keep busy but that coping at work was a great strain. Fathers whose work brings them into contact with large numbers of people (for example, teachers or local government officers) found such constant contact difficult and nearly all fathers found concentration and problem-solving very difficult for the first few weeks after their baby's death. When one father first returned to work after his son's death he found that: 'I had had enough and needed to digest it my own way. I did this by having a week of going to work, arriving and then just leaving. I spent the time driving around the countryside and walking but in a daze (I drove over eighty miles one day, I've no idea where).'

Whilst work can serve to take the father's mind off his grief, there is a risk that it will simply postpone expression of the grief, which will then have to be faced and handled at a later date. In our own case, my husband Pat became very withdrawn and for a year I watched him helplessly, driving himself ever harder at work in an attempt to cope with the grief he could not express. The very closeness that we have always enjoyed in our happy marriage enabled us to comfort and support each other in many ways but it made talking about Elizabeth impossible. We were too raw; it couldn't be done. Ultimately it was a chance encounter a year later that helped Pat most. He had met a fellow steam-train enthusiast and I had left them chatting together one evening while I went to a cookery class (my way of trying to pick up the threads and start meeting people again). I returned to find them both in tears, having just discovered that it was not only a love of trains which they had in common. His friend had also lost a baby in a cot death, incredibly in our own town and on the same day as that of our daughter's death. When, some years later, I mentioned that evening of shared grieving to Pat, he had no memory of it, so obviously the pain had been severe enough for him to block it all out, but I know that it helped him at the time because it gave him the opening he had needed for his own grieving to be given expression.

Coping at work can be very difficult. As one father pointed out: 'Everything seemed so trivial and I was on a short fuse.' A cot death changes our whole attitude to life; we discover new priorities and discard old ones. As a result, it is not only attitudes to work which are affected. Cliff used to like going with his mates to shoot rabbits, but after his son Christopher died in a cot death at the age of 7 weeks, he could not enjoy the outings any more: 'Me and me mate went shooting the other day but when I saw a rabbit in my sights I deliberately aimed to one side – I know now, life's too precious.'

(9) *Would you have found a fathers' support group helpful?*

Naturally everyone responded differently to this question, but some felt that a fathers' group might have been helpful as it would have released them from the pressure of being the strong one in front of their partner and would have allowed them to show their vulnerability and share their grief. One father felt that it would be difficult to share his emotions with other men, and another pointed out that attending a fathers' group, like attending a Study Day, might simply bring back the grief and make coping more difficult.

(10) *Were you allowed to see your baby after death had occurred and if so, did this help or would you have preferred not to do so?*

The fathers who saw and held their babies immediately after death found this helpful to them. Those who were not present at the time or not given the chance to hold their baby and say goodbye later regretted it.

(11) *Did you choose burial or cremation and, whichever you chose, do you feel that it was the right decision?*

This was a practical question as I wanted to be able to offer advice to other families faced with similar decisions to make. As expected, answers varied. One father accepted his wife's decision to opt for cremation but later felt the need for a grave as a focal point, somewhere to go to grieve, whilst another advised against having a grave because of the difficulty of letting go if there is a grave to visit. What did come across was that, where well-meaning relatives had taken charge and made the funeral arrangements, bereaved fathers had regretted their lost opportunity of involvement, which emphasizes the point made elsewhere that parents should be encouraged to reach their own decisions and take an active part in arrangements.

(12) *For those of you who have had a subsequent baby, did this re-*

open old griefs and fears, or had they passed by then, or were they there anyway but not increased by the new baby?

As expected, responses varied, but all those with a subsequent baby agreed that the grief was there anyway and that the fear of another cot death remained very great. 'I don't believe the fear will ever leave me. I shall worry about my children and probably theirs, too.' For some, weighing and monitoring proved very helpful. Others preferred to go it alone, although one father caused consternation to passers-by in the middle of town by suddenly, during a panic-attack, slapping his baby daughter across the face to rouse her, because she had failed to respond when her toe was pinched. All that had happened was that 'the poor child had dropped off into a deep sleep' but panic and fear are never far away from those who have experienced a cot death.

(13) *Did you have a preference for the sex of the subsequent baby and if so, did this alter once the new baby had established his or her own personality?*

Most fathers were simply relieved to have a healthy subsequent baby. Some expressed disappointment if the next baby proved to be of the opposite sex to the baby who had died, followed by a sense of relief that there could be no risk of comparisons or living up to the dead baby's image and a profound love for the new baby in his or her own right.

(14) *According to the experts, bereaved parents pass through certain well defined stages of grief – numbing, then disbelief, then disorganization (where everything seems to fall apart) and then reorganization and recovery. Would you say that this has been true where you yourself are concerned?*

This provoked quite strong reactions, with most fathers pointing out that human nature is too variable and complex for stages of grieving to be in any way rigidly defined. 'There are different stages to grieving but they are not as separate and as clear-cut as the textbooks would make you think. You can slip back to earlier stages as well as moving forward.'

(15) *Asking questions is very restricting, so is there anything that you would like to say which hasn't been covered by the questions above?*

Most fathers left this section blank, which may mean that they were simply exhausted by then! Hopefully, on the other hand, it may mean that the main aspects had been covered by the other questions. One father added information by enclosing an article which he had written for TAMBA's bereavement group *Newsletter*, plus a copy of an interview which he and his wife had given to *Essentials* magazine, and he thereby raised an important point. Many fathers want to express their feelings, what they need is an opening to do so. From the very moving answers which I received to my questionnaire, if nothing else it provided just such an opportunity and I felt very privileged to be the recipient of such full and honest replies.

(16) *What single piece of advice would you pass on to other fathers who find themselves having to cope with the tragedy of a cot death?*

Some fathers did not feel qualified to give any advice, since cot death is such a personal experience, but two replies stand out: 'People will tell you that a mother's grief is different from a father's. Perhaps they are right but that is not the whole story. Everybody's grief is different. You have a right to grieve in your own way.'

'You'll never get over the anguish and sense of loss but these feelings diminish with time and providing you can have, or have got, other children, then they will help. But never accept the saying: "life goes on, and you should stop grieving now." It does. You won't.'

4

What About the Baby's Brothers and Sisters?

Breaking the news

Breaking the news of the baby's death to other children in the family is very difficult indeed, but much unnecessary suffering can be avoided if parents can bring themselves to be honest and open about the baby's death and to tell their other children as quickly and as accurately as possible. Delays tend to undermine children's confidence in their parents and can lead to problems such as phobias. Parents need to emphasize that the doctor and/or the hospital did all that was possible, to avoid the risk of children developing a dislike and fear of their doctor or of hospitals at a future date.

Often other children in the family are present at the time of the discovery. Faced with a reality which they cannot fully understand, these children will find it even harder than adults do to accept that the baby is dead forever and can never return to life. Physical contact is very important at such a time and most children will need to be cuddled and comforted. On the other hand, if a child wishes to be alone to cope with the shock, then these wishes should be respected. Be guided by your children and by your own instincts.

At the time when the baby is found dead, the shock and grief are so overwhelming that it can be almost impossible to realize how other children in the house must be feeling and to answer their needs when your own are so great. If you are unable to cope, ask a relative or friend to help, because your other children will need an immense amount of comforting and reassurance. At a single blow they have not only lost their younger brother or sister, in a sense they have also temporarily lost their parents, together with all that they have known in the way of home life and security. The parents that they thought were strong and all-powerful suddenly seem like lost children themselves, deeply distressed and helpless in the face of what has happened. This threatens the very root of security and stability for the remaining children, so no wonder they feel so bewildered and confused.

Coping with shock and anger

As with parents, the first reaction of other children is that of shock. Children are often easy to distract and it may be tempting to use this as a solution, but distraction does not remove their reaction, it simply postpones it. The best response to shock remains that of warmth and rest, close physical comforting followed by a quiet period in bed, if this is what the child wishes. Younger children may appreciate a cuddly toy or hot water bottle to hold. Older children may appreciate the physical closeness and attention of an adult and may even accept a hot water bottle without damage to their fragile pride. It is only too easy for brothers and sisters to feel very lonely and isolated at such a time, so if possible try to encourage them to feel useful once the initial shock has passed. It can also help if you are able to provide outlets for their very natural subsequent feelings of anger and aggression. Tearing up cardboard boxes can be very therapeutic! Physical activities such as vacuuming, sweeping the yard or washing the car can channel and defuse violent emotions and make the children feel useful and valued at a time when they may be feeling guilty simply for still being alive when the much-loved baby is dead.

On the morning of 13 October 1982, Jill went to wake her 18-month-old son Duncan and found him dead in his cot. Her 4-year-old daughter Helen was with her at the time. Just under a month later, Jill heard Helen reciting a poem of her own invention to herself, chanting it over and over again. Helen continued to chant the poem for a number of days afterwards and Jill decided to write down what Helen was saying:

> The flowers in the fields
> We pick for our mums
> Who keep them 'til they die
> And then they go in the rubbish.
> Everything that's real dies.
> Flowers die. Cows die.

It can be helpful to encourage children to express their feelings through writing, drawing, painting or even acting, which may permit them to say and do things which they might otherwise feel would not be allowed. Expressing themselves creatively can be very cathartic and it is an area where their school can be of great help, if their teacher is wise, experienced and able to cope with the emotions which may be stirred up and released. Allowing expression of the emotions caused by a death can be of benefit to the whole class, who may be wondering how best to help their bereaved friend and also how to come to terms with their own feelings. For such expression to be successful, much will depend on the teacher's relationship with the bereaved child and on the teacher's ability to guide and control the situation in class.

Children at school can be very cruel at such a time, for this is their way of handling a situation which threatens their own security. They may well be thinking: 'If his brother or sister can die, perhaps others can as well . . . perhaps mine. Perhaps me.' Adults need to be aware of the hurtful comments and behaviour with which their already distressed child may be having to cope: 'I'm not surprised your baby died. I would die as well if I had to have *you* as a brother/sister.' 'Your baby's dead, isn't she, she's in the ground and worms are eating her all up.' Images of the baby's body after burial are upsetting enough for parents – for children they can be devastating, which is why it is so important to explain clearly and simply the implications of cremation or burial; otherwise, the images suggested by young schoolfriends may prove to be even worse.

Visiting the baby after death and attending the funeral

If the baby looks peaceful and normal, then it may help if your other children are allowed to visit their brother or sister in the chapel of rest or funeral parlour, but do check first to ensure that their baby will look as they would want him or her to look and never force children to go who do not wish to do so. If they were present when the baby was discovered they may well have a very distressing image in their mind. Often the process of death means that the baby's face will have become flattened, distorted and discoloured and this can be a horrific memory which can take a long time to fade, so to see the baby later looking peaceful can do much to reduce the distress caused by the earlier image. It must be remembered, however, that the peaceful-looking baby in the chapel of rest or funeral parlour will be very cold to the touch and some children may be very upset if make-up has been employed to make the baby look as 'natural' as possible, so your children will need to be well informed and prepared before making any decision.

The decision as to whether other children in the family should visit the baby after death and later attend the funeral service is one which they and their parents should make together. If the children feel able to cope, experience has shown that seeing the baby again and attending the funeral does help to reinforce the reality of the baby's death, thereby helping the other children to come to terms with what has happened. Small children are confused by the disappearance of the baby rather than by the baby's death. When they are too young to understand the concept of death, it is the disappearance that worries them most because they are left wondering who will disappear next. Similarly a child who sees his or her baby brother or sister rushed away in an ambulance, and is then left with no explanation and no proof of the baby's death, may well harbour fantasies that the baby will return at a future date and such fantasies can be very damaging. 'If only I can make myself good enough, perhaps he/she will be allowed to come back.'

When cot death strikes, bereaved parents know only too well the feeling that 'this is a nightmare, it must be, please God let me wake up and find it isn't true'. For children this feeling can be just as powerful, perhaps even more so if they are still at the age of magical thinking where they believe that their actions and wishes can influence events. We excluded Rebecca from the funeral and we realize now that it was probably a mistake. We had wanted to spare her the ordeal, but as a result she was left totally baffled as to where Elizabeth had gone. I could not bring myself to explain the implications of cremation to a 4-year-old when I was finding them so hard to accept myself, so Rebecca was left to draw muddled conclusions which probably only added to her already existing state of confusion. Sooner or later, painful realities have to be faced. If parents and their surviving children can face them together, there is more chance that the pain of grief can be successfully handled and overcome and healing allowed to begin.

How children cope with grief

Because children cannot always express themselves in the way that they would wish, they are likely to express their reactions, emotions and fears through their behaviour. It can be very distressing to parents to find their children 'playing funerals', using a doll as the dead baby, but this may be a vital step for them in coming to terms with what has happened. As a bereaved parent, it may seem to you that your other children are being especially demanding and difficult just when you most need them to behave well and take some of the pressure away from you, not add to it. Just when you feel least able to cope, you find yourself being challenged and tested to the limit. 'Can I have her clothes now she's dead, they'll fit my big doll?' – one gauntlet thrown down with awesome accuracy, and likely to be only one of many. The messages are there loud and clear, but dealing with them can be very difficult and emotionally draining.

Becky, like most 9-year-old girls, used to enjoy playing with her Sindy dolls and Sindy house. When her younger sister Jessica died in a cot death at the age of 16 months, Becky gathered together all her dolls, ranging from Sindies and Barbies down to Sylvanian and other small figures, and she set them up in the different rooms in her Sindy house. She placed them in groups of four and in each group she laid the smallest doll face down on the floor. Children do not always need words to speak very eloquently about their feelings. Becky's groups of dolls stayed undisturbed until she announced that she would like her Sindy house to be packed away as she no longer wanted to play with it. As if symbolically packing away her childhood as well, Becky and her mother then cleared all the dolls and put both them and the house away. In true mothering fashion, however, Becky took on responsibility for Jessica's favourite doll, tucking the doll into bed beside her own large and much-loved doll and caring for her on Jessica's behalf. Five months after Jessica's death, Becky sorted through all the toys which she had been saving for her sister and gave them instead to her grandparents to keep for other visiting children. Becky had acknowledged the reality of Jessica's death and the stark fact that Jessica would never be able to play with the toys which she had been keeping for her.

If parents can be forewarned of likely reactions in their children, it can help to reduce the distress such reactions may provoke and encourage understanding and tolerance. It used to be thought that young children did not feel the full effects of grief following a death, but it is now well recognized that they do, simply that they may not be able to communicate their grief through language. Instead they use behaviour and it is very common for toddlers and even older children to revert to infantile ways – regressing in toilet training, bed-wetting and waking during the night, experiencing nightmares and demanding to be treated like a baby during the day (by, for example, being spoon-fed again and by clinging very closely to their mother or any other adult who happens to be present at the time). These children need extra love whenever possible, with plenty of cuddling and reassurance to re-establish some sense of security.

Parents and relatives can help their children by making daily life as structured and as regular as possible, since this will assist in restoring their damaged security. Surviving children will be only too aware that their parents are wanting their dead baby all the time. This can make them feel that they are not good enough, for they know that being there themselves obviously is not enough to make their parents happy. They can feel very inadequate because they are unable to comfort their grieving parents and very burdened by the role-reversal which the cot death has placed upon them. Trying to support the parents they once thought invincible is no easy task and children can be worrying about their parents and grieving for them as well as for themselves.

In response to the death of their baby brother or sister, some children may become aggressive and deliberately misbehave, whilst others may become withdrawn and behave too well, possibly from a fear that if they do anything wrong they will die as well, as a punishment. Those children who appear to be unaffected and even callous in fact tend to be the most seriously affected, for they are likely to be repressing a pain too great for them to acknowledge and handle and they are likely to suffer more lasting damage as a result, including the risk of being overwhelmed by grief at a later age over something that does not seem to warrant such an extreme reaction.

Even though it is now acknowledged that young children can and do feel profound grief, there is another, special category of child who may be overlooked, that of the surviving twin in a cot-death tragedy. Twins are known to be at higher risk of cot death than single babies. When one twin dies, the surviving twin is likely to sense the loss and to grieve, no matter how young he or she may be at the time. Parents talk of their surviving babies sometimes refusing to eat and sometimes refusing to sleep afterwards, or alternatively lapsing into an almost comatose sleep as a reaction. They speak of them being distressed and difficult to comfort and sometimes appearing to become ill. As surviving twins remain at high risk of suffering a similar death for about a month following the first death, it may be necessary to hospitalize them for a close watch to be kept on their condition. This can create problems of its own, unfortunately, with the extra stress imposed by separation from parents, home and security. Even if they remain at home, their handling may suffer a deterioration while their parents are so engulfed by their own grief.

Even though I was not aware of it at the time and thought that I was behaving normally and coping all right, I realize now that much of Mary's babyhood is a blank to me. I remember only too well the very real fear that she would also die and I am aware that this fear can affect the parenting of the surviving twin. Since there is no time for parents to adjust and to mourn in the way that parents would usually do before embarking on another pregnancy and baby, this too can have an effect on how the growing twin is handled. If parents can be aware of this, it may help them when coping with their surviving twin whilst mourning the twin who has died.

Some children react physically to the baby's death by developing new conditions or accentuating existing conditions such as asthma, eczema or hay fever. They may develop rashes, headaches or even stammers and their resistance to childhood ailments is likely to be lowered while they are grieving. Older children may experience problems such as anorexia, insomnia and hallucinations and parents will need to be sensitive to such possibilities as the youngsters themselves may be reluctant to acknowledge or talk about what they are experiencing.

Older sisters (and often brothers as well) of about 7 upwards often adopt the role of 'other mother' and can grieve in a similar way to the mother herself when the baby suddenly dies. They need to be allowed to grieve fully so as not to spoil their later role in life as parents of their own future children.

When a major catastrophe or any natural disaster involving much loss of life occurs, adults often feel a compulsion to spread and to share the distressing news as quickly as possible. In just the same way, young children, too, may feel an overwhelming need to tell everyone, including strangers in the street, that their baby brother or sister has died. They may seem to enjoy the dangerous potency and power attached to the giving of such news but it is also an effective way of trying to come to terms with what has happened.

Following a cot death in their family, school-age children often suffer a loss of confidence and this, combined with the likelihood of a temporary inability to concentrate, often means that their school work will suffer for a while. Teachers and parents can help by taking an extra interest in their work and by doing everything possible to restore their confidence in themselves.

Grief, fear and guilt

After the baby's death, children are likely to have to cope with three dominant and difficult emotions: grief, fear and guilt. If they are to recover, we have to give them not only permission to acknowledge these feelings but also great support in working through them. The best advice is not new but it still holds true: help with your heart, not your head.

It is sometimes difficult for adults to appreciate what may be going through the minds of their children when their baby dies. Young children may well believe that they have caused the baby's death, especially if they were the first in the room and tried unsuccessfully to wake the baby. It is very important to emphasize to children that they did *not* cause the death and that they will not die as well, for they may not always feel able to tell of their fears.

At a young age children cannot comprehend the permanence of death and may therefore upset their parents deeply by repeatedly asking when the dead baby is going to return. It is essential for adults to be plain and honest about what has happened, for it is all too easy for children to misunderstand what adults are saying to them. If they are mistakenly told that their baby has 'gone to sleep', this can make them afraid ever to risk sleeping soundly again and can lead to night terrors. If they are told: 'We've lost our baby,' or overhear their parents saying so, is it any wonder that some react by going to look for the baby who is missing, unwittingly adding to their parents' distress?

Young children have great difficulty in understanding the terminology used by adults. If they are told that the baby's body will be buried, some are likely to be left wondering what will happen to the arms and the legs. Many parents, myself included, find it deeply distressing to discuss the implications of cremation and burial, and yet it is only by being as honest and straightforward as possible that painful misunderstandings can be avoided. The questions which your other children ask are likely unintentionally to hurt, but they are very important to the children, so try if possible to hear both what is being asked and why it is being asked and then do all you can to answer simply and truthfully. If you do not know what happens after death, say so, for children will soon sense if you are trying to give them a belief which you do not yourself feel to be true. Even if you have a firm and supportive belief in heaven, try to avoid the popular idea that: 'Jesus wanted our baby for a sunbeam,' as a solution, for this is no solution at all because it leaves the surviving children with two very worrying alternatives: either Jesus does *not* want them, which can lead to a sense of rejection, or Jesus *does* want them, which can lead to a very real fear that they, too, may be struck by a similar death at any time.

At the 1981 Study Day in Sheffield, I heard Dr Mary Lindsay, child psychiatrist, give a very valuable talk on the affects of cot death on older children. How I wish I had been able to hear her in 1979 – I might have avoided so many mistakes! She pointed out that children under the age of 5 are still experiencing an age of magical thinking, so that their very vivid imaginations can allow fantasies to take over; for them, dreams can be as real as reality. They can suffer from intense anxiety and also from intense anger, which can be very damaging. At that age, children may tend to blame their parents, or indeed themselves, remembering the times that their natural but strong jealousy has prompted them to wish that the baby would die or go away. Everything seems to conspire against them. Their mother becomes pregnant and is preoccupied, so they receive less attention and may well feel rejected. Then she goes away to hospital, compounding the sense of loss and rejection and then, to add insult to injury, she returns with a new baby who commands most of her love and time. Even though the older child wants to love the new baby, feelings of hate can also be very strong. When the baby dies suddenly and unexpectedly, the older child's worst fears and fantasies are realized.

According to Dr Lindsay, an older child can use words like 'dead' and 'died' without understanding them. Apparently, a child cannot accept that death is permanent until he or she is 9, and cannot fully understand all the implications of death until the age of 11, with the result that children often 'deep freeze' their reactions until they are old enough to cope with them, with the result that their very genuine distress may not surface until early teens or beyond. If as parents, members of the family or family friends, you can be aware of these potential problems, it may help you to understand the needs and the fears of older children and to answer their questions as simply and as honestly as possible.

Offering help

Immediately after the baby's death, when everything is in turmoil, it can be very tempting to accept offers from relatives or friends and send the other child or children to them to spare them some of the distress which they will be seeing all around them at home. Try, if possible, to resist this temptation because what you see as a kindness, your children may see as a rejection. They need to grieve with their own family at home and they need to see their family grieve for the baby. For the mourning to be worked through successfully, it helps if it can be a shared experience. Although it is natural to want to protect your children from pain, it is necessary for them to be allowed to acknowledge and show their very real sadness, since they, too, have to work through it. Don't try to protect them from this because it has to be faced, but do give them your support, with as much love and attention as possible.

If your own pain is so great that you cannot answer the needs of your other children, then enlist the help of relatives, friends or professional counsellors. Doctors can often seem too busy, but Child Guidance Clinics are available and can offer skilled, non-judgemental help and support. You can contact one of these clinics either directly or via your doctor or health visitor. You need not fear that it will imply that there is anything 'wrong' with your child or children; the clinics are there to help and can offer valuable guidance through the very natural process of grieving. It must be remembered that, although a child's period of intense grief may be shorter, the full grieving period may last longer than an adult's because of the increasing understanding which develops during childhood, giving fresh insights and renewing the grief that is felt.

Friends and family can do much to comfort the other child or children when a cot death shatters their world, but they must be careful about what they say and do if they are to avoid causing unintentional harm. Try to avoid common phrases such as: 'You must be a brave little man and not cry,' or 'You must help your Mummy and Daddy because they're very upset,' – so too is the child. He or she needs to mourn as well and to have his or her own feelings recognized and respected.

Because the pain is so real, many relatives and friends try to deny the previous existence of the baby and avoid any mention of the name when the other children are present, but this is not a solution. The baby remains a member of the family even though he or she is no longer with them. It can help if a photograph of the baby can be displayed at home because this can reinforce the reality of the baby and allow the other children to speak of their dead brother or sister and to ask the questions which may be worrying them but which they would not otherwise feel able to mention.

Knowing how you yourself feel, try to recognize what your children are feeling. Like the mourning of adults, there are no strictly set patterns, but children are likely to pass through certain phases of grief – shock, denial, searching, despair, anger, anxiety and guilt – all of which can culminate in a very real depression. I can see now that our 4-year-old daughter Rebecca suffered very deep grief reactions when her sister died, but at the time I was so engulfed by my own grief that I was more aware of the behaviour problems which she presented and which we found difficult to handle. She lost interest in her food and often refused to eat the meals I had prepared. I took this as a rejection of my care and many battles ensued which could have been avoided if I had realized what she was doing and why she was doing it. I tried very hard to give her as much attention as possible, despite my own depression and the demands of her surviving baby sister Mary. It was not easy. If I praised any picture which she had drawn, she would immediately scribble through it and destroy it. I had a very distressed little child in the house and at times I felt powerless to help her. She wanted to love Mary. When I breastfed Mary, Rebecca would pull down the front of her summer dresses and breastfeed her doll to keep me company, but the grief which we were both feeling for Elizabeth constantly threatened to overwhelm us. In trying to protect her from the pain, I unintentionally excluded her. On the one occasion when she found me sobbing in a heap, she put her arm round me to comfort me, saying: 'Don't cry, Mummy.' Her arm was so small, it seemed so wrong for her to be carrying such a burden that I vowed never to let her catch me crying again, not realizing that she *needed* to grieve with me and *needed* to offer me comfort. From then on I used to wait until she was at playgroup before letting the tears come and as a result, Rebecca was left with no openings for her own emotions, no chance to talk and to ask all the questions that were worrying her. Hiding my emotions consequently suppressed hers as well, so that they were driven underground and took a long, long time to surface again.

Grieving is hard work, both for parents and for their children. For the grieving to have a successful outcome there are no short cuts and no escape routes – these merely postpone, they don't remove. Inevitably cot death imposes immense stress on a family and sadly some families will find themselves torn apart by the consequences.

WHAT ABOUT THE BABY'S BROTHERS AND SISTERS?

On the other hand, a cot death can also, if worked through together as a family, lead to very strong bonds, drawing the family very close together, arming them well against any future stresses and problems and uniting them in a deep appreciation of the value of family ties and family life.

5

Families and Friends

In some ways a cot death can be compared to an earthquake that suddenly hits a town without warning. The buildings at the centre, those most likely to suffer severe damage, are the baby's parents, brothers and sisters. If they are built to cope with such an extreme event then they will survive the impact and in time the damage will be reparable, but as buildings they will never be quite the same again. As the earthquake ripples outwards it will hit the next area of buildings – the grandparents and relatives. Learning that such a young and precious member of their family has died so unexpectedly and inexplicably hits with all the impact of an earthquake. If these buildings, too, are built to cope then they will also survive and be able to undergo repair but, even though they are further from the epicentre, any weakness in structure (such as ill health or poor previous family relationships) will increase the danger of damage which may be severe, long-lasting and possibly irreparable. The further away from the centre such buildings stand, the less likely they are to suffer severe damage, but few will remain unaffected. The ambulance and hospital staff, the police, coroner's officer, coroner and registrar, the doctor, health visitor, midwife and paediatrician, the minister of religion, funeral director and funeral staff – all will feel the impact of the earthquake and to a lesser or greater degree be affected by it.

Both cot deaths and earthquakes are unpredictable and unpreventable. We know that possible risk factors exist in certain babies, just as we know that certain earthquake zones exist in the world. It makes sense to reduce the risk factors in babies if at all possible, just as it makes sense to avoid living in an earthquake zone or at least to build structures most capable of withstanding the effects if an earthquake strikes, but in both cases the tragedy can happen where and when least expected and the damage caused can be immense.

Grandparents

Grandparents have an especially difficult burden to bear. They experience a double grief, for not only do they have to try and cope with the loss of their grandchild, they also have to witness the suffering of their own adult child and in such a situation they can feel very helpless. It sometimes happens that the closer the grandparent and adult child have been before the death, the more difficult they will find it to share and talk about their mutual loss and grief afterwards and great tolerance, understanding and sensitivity are required on both sides.

At the time of the baby's death, it is natural for cot-death parents to revert to feeling like helpless children again and to seek the support and reassurance of their parents, even though such parents may be elderly and in failing health. It is a very primitive response which makes us silently plead: 'Tell me it's all a bad dream, put it right for me,' even though the adult part of us knows that this is not possible.

When Andrew's wife Joss found their 10-week-old twin son Peter not breathing properly, Andrew at first felt: '. . . strangely detached and yet compelled into action, as if performing a role in some pre-ordained drama. In this state I called for an ambulance, sent for a neighbour and began to give Peter the kiss of life. Settling into some sort of rhythm gave me more time to think . . . I began to worry whether I was getting the mouth-to-mouth right. I wasn't. There was an awful gurgling sound and then green bilge surged out through his uncovered nose. I was horrified, convinced I had experienced his death throes. I went to pieces completely. Panic set in. Ridiculously I left him to Joss and our neighbour and rushed downstairs to phone my mother. She was too far away to be of any help but I was desperate and needed my mother as I had not since I was a small boy. I had scarcely had time to speak to and worry her before the ambulance came.'

Peter was given all the attention and devotion of his parents, the ambulance and casualty staff and the staff of the Special Care Baby Unit, plus all the advantages of modern medical technology, but sadly it was not enough and after twenty-four hours he lost his tentative hold on life.

No wonder, at such a time, that many of us feel a deep need to turn to our parents for comfort. This can prove difficult for grandparents to handle if they live a long way away or if they have become used to their adult child leading a separate and independent life. Suddenly the grandmother is thrown back into her mothering and nurturing role, just when she is least expecting it and at the time when her own grief is at its most intense and difficult to handle.

Grandparents grieve very deeply for their dead grandchild and it can be a problem for cot-death parents, in the midst of their profound loss, to recognize that their own parents need comfort and support as well.

One grandmother found that her daughter became very dependent on her again, coming to her house every day to weep and to talk about her little girl who'd just died in a cot death at the age of 5½ months. The grandmother recognized that this was a vital outlet for her daughter and allowed her full freedom to come, but found her visits emotionally very draining. In the ultra-sensitive state that often follows a bereavement, her daughter was quick to mis-interpret words that were intended to help and often vented much of her inward anger and frustration against her mother, who said that at times: 'I felt like a punchbag.' Eventually, after an exhausting and distressing scene, the grandmother spoke out to her daughter and said: 'Don't you think I'm grieving, too, that it's hard for me as well?' This gave her daughter an insight into her mother's suffering which up until that time she had not been able to recognize, and from then on they were more able to grieve together and share the burden.

One of the predominant emotions after a cot death is guilt. Parents agonize over what they did or failed to do prior to their baby's death. Grandparents can sometimes feel guilty simply for still being alive. 'Young babies shouldn't die, it isn't right. I'm old and it should be me who's dead instead.' Even more than others, they can feel that the natural order of events has been broken, since death should come at the end of a full life, not at the beginning of it.

Grandparents are the least likely to have heard about cot death. They will often be tempted to say: 'This didn't happen in my young day.' It did, but at that time it was not recognized as a cause of death and therefore the term 'sudden infant death' did not appear on death certificates. When our grandparents were young, more babies and small children died than is now the case and they did so from a variety of causes which, because of medical advances, have since been eradicated (illnesses such as diptheria, tetanus, polio, tuberculosis etc.). It is because these causes of death have been reduced that the cot death syndrome now shows so clearly, but it has always existed and the rate has always remained approximately the same. The main difference is that at one time, doctors faced with having to give a cause of death on the death certificate had to resort to vague terms such as bronchiolitis, whereas since 1979 they have been allowed to recognize SIDS as a cause of death and to name it on the certificate.

Where grandparents have never heard about SIDS, the urge to find fault in whichever parent was caring for the baby at the time must be very strong – after all, isn't it exactly what we as parents do to ourselves when our baby dies? To prevent this temptation from arising, it can be helpful for bereaved parents to obtain a copy of the leaflet: *Information for Parents following the Sudden and Un-expected Death of their Baby*, and to show it to grandparents, relatives and friends as an explanation for the baby's death. The leaflet is available free from the FSID which has also tried to ensure that copies are available at surgeries, health centres and offices of registrars throughout the country.

Family relationships

A baby's sudden death is a tragic loss for everyone – the parents, brothers and sisters, grandparents, aunt, uncles, cousins . . . the larger the family, the more people there are who have to try and cope with the affects of bereavement. It is a very difficult and emotional time and the impact of the cot death will tend either to draw family relationships closer together or to blow them wide apart, depending upon the quality of these relationships before-hand. No one remains unchanged. When families are able to grieve together and offer mutual support, then they can emerge from the tragedy stronger and more united than ever. Unfortunately the shock of a cot death can act as a catalyst and bring to the surface many underlying family tensions and feuds, which can then increase the stress of an already extremely stressful situation. Sadly, the very time which should unite families can be the time when hostilities erupt, so as family members do be prepared for such consequences and do try not to instigate them if they can possibly be avoided. Problems usually arise when relatives have very strong views on how to respond and act following the cot death. Clashes over funeral arrangements are not uncommon and it is unrealistic to hope that the arrangements which are chosen will answer every-one's needs. Compromise is essential, and it helps if everyone can remember that there are no right or wrong responses to a cot death, only natural ones. Try not to feel hurt or outraged if a relative responds in a way which seems totally alien to you. We all have to grieve in our own way and what is appropriate for one person may not be appropriate for another. In the weeks and months following the baby's death, much tolerance and understanding will be required by all concerned if rifts are to be avoided and family relationships encouraged not just to survive intact but also to develop and mature.

Friends and acquaintances

Often family and friends are only too anxious to help but feel totally at a loss as to how to do so. They can help in a practical way, of course, by cooking meals and doing the washing or the shopping, but if they are willing to do so they can also help in an emotional way, by giving bereaved families the openings they need in order to talk about what has happened. It takes a true and brave friend to do this and I have heard of friends crossing the road to avoid bereaved parents, not as a form of rejection or implied blame but simply because they did not know what to say. Most take the easy option and talk about everything *but* the baby who has died.

For relatives and friends to be of help to you as bereaved parents, it will be necessary for you to be very honest about your feelings. They will be so afraid of unintentionally upsetting you that it will be up to you to guide them and to say either: 'This is how I'm feeling today. Please let me talk about our baby,' or 'Today I'm feeling too raw even to speak our baby's name so please can we talk about other subjects and not mention cot deaths at all.' On the other hand, as bereaved parents you may well find yourself trying to protect your relatives and friends from the inevitable pain which follows a cot death and may spend your time trying to 'spare' them instead of answering your own needs. Sparing is not possible. Grief has to be worked through by everyone involved. By allowing yourselves to share your grief with your family and friends, you will be giving them permission to grieve as well.

The Compassionate Friends, an organization of bereaved parents, has published a very valuable list of DOs and DON'Ts to guide people about helpful and unhelpful reactions:

DOs	*DON'Ts*
DO let your genuine concern and caring show	DON'T let your own sense of helplessness keep you from reaching out to a bereaved parent
DO be available . . . to listen, to run errands, to help with the other children, or whatever else seems needed at the time	DON'T avoid them because you are uncomfortable (being avoided by friends adds pain to an already intolerably painful experience)
DO say you are sorry about what happened to their child and about their pain	DON'T say how you know how they feel (unless you've lost a child yourself you probably don't know how they feel)
DO allow them to express as much grief as they are feeling at the moment and are willing to share	
DO encourage them to be patient with themselves, not to expect too much of themselves and not to impose any 'shoulds' on themselves	DON'T say 'you ought to be feeling better by now' or anything else which implies a judgement about their feelings
DO allow them to talk about the child they have lost as much and as often as they want to	DON'T tell them what they *should* feel or do
	DON'T change the subject when they mention their dead child
DO talk about the special endearing qualities of the child they've lost	DON'T avoid mentioning the child's name out of fear of reminding them of their pain (they haven't forgotten it!)
DO give special attention to the child's brothers and sisters – at the funeral and in the months to come (they too are hurt and confused and in need of attention which their parents may not be able to give at this time)	DON'T try to find something positive (e.g. a moral lesson, closer family ties, etc.) about the child's death
	DON'T point out at least they have their other children (children are not interchangeable; they cannot replace each other)

DO reassure them that they did everything that they could, that the medical care their child received was the best or whatever else you know to be *true and positive* about the care given to their child

DON'T say that they can always have another child (even if they wanted to and could, another child would not replace the child they've lost)

DON'T suggest that they should be grateful for their other children (grief over the loss of one child does not discount parent's love and appreciation of their living children)

DON'T make any comments which in any way suggest that the care given their child at home, in the emergency department, hospital, or whatever, was inadequate (parents are plagued by feelings of doubt and guilt without any help from their family and friends)

Prepared by Lee Schmidt, Parent Bereavement Outreach, Santa Monica, California, and reproduced by courtesy of the Compassionate Friends.

Ignorance and misinformation

One of the greatest problems surrounding cot death is ignorance. The FSID has achieved a great deal in informing the public about the nature of cot deaths but old prejudices linger on and you are still likely to encounter those who genuinely believe that you are to blame, either through something you did or something you failed to do in the way of care or, worse still, through actively causing your baby's death by deliberate smothering. 'Gentle battering' it has been called and it only needs the occasional 'expert' to speak without any basis of facts for the media to seize upon the opportunity for horrendous headline news coverage. The harm which this causes is incalculable, causing even the sanest of mothers to ask themselves: 'Could I have done so without knowing it? Did I sleepwalk in the night and smother my dearly loved baby?' I suppose those of us whose babies died while others were present should consider ourselves fortunate, but such ill-informed publicity simply reinforces the deep feelings of guilt which already exist. In our rational minds we know that there is nothing that we could have done to prevent the death and that we are not to blame in any way, but in our hearts we feel that we *must* be to blame because common sense dictates that healthy, well-protected babies don't suddenly die for no reason.

Thoughtless remarks from friends, family or acquaintances can cause deep distress to cot-death parents, who inevitably feel vulnerable for a long time after their baby has died. Please think very carefully before suggesting possible causes to bereaved parents – they will already be searching around for sticks with which to beat themselves, they don't need to be handed any more. When self-confidence is already shattered, it does not help if well-meaning friends suggest: 'Perhaps it was the type of cot/carrycot/pram you used, or the brand of milk/baby food you used . . .' Try and remember how many thousands of babies use similar types of equipment or brands of food and survive without difficulty, and be wary of passing on unsubstantiated and often misleading and distressing media reports.

I can well remember one occasion on which I lost my temper and spoke out. I was helping to run a cot-death tombola stall at Hickstead, in Sussex. I had already learnt that, although the prizes to be won would come in for close scrutiny, those of us offering them would remain mysteriously invisible to passers-by, but I had not realized that we were supposed to be deaf, too. A very loud woman walking past, glanced at our appeal poster and announced confidently and arrogantly: 'But we all know what causes cot deaths. They're caused by bottle-feeding.' I had worked so hard to ensure that our twins were breastfed, hiring a milk-expressing machine called a 'humilactor' while they were in the Special Care Unit at hospital and using it every three hours, including during the night, to ensure that my supply would establish and then keep pace with both of them, ready for the time when they would no longer need to be fed through a tube and could take their milk directly from me. I loathed that machine. What I wanted so much was to be holding my babies in my arms and giving my milk to them, not to a wretched mechanical contraption. The woman's sweeping state-ment hit a very raw nerve indeed and I leapt from behind the stall and accosted her verbally, explaining that my daughter who had died had been 99 per cent breastfed and that many 100 per cent breastfed babies had also died in cot deaths. As I spoke, she visibly shrank before me and I felt instantly guilty. To do her credit, when I had finished my outburst she gave a generous donation. I still wince at my action but I don't regret it. Ignorance is no excuse – if you are not absolutely sure of your facts, it is best to keep your theories to yourself. Uninformed and tactless remarks can be very hurtful and damaging.

On the other hand, wise and compassionate support from family, friends and acquaintances can be of invaluable help. Yes, it will be time-consuming and, yes, it will be emotionally draining. There is only so much that family and friends, with stresses and commitments of their own, can take in the way of dependence and tears on the part of the bereaved parent seeking their help, but the more that they are prepared to give of their time and their willingness to listen (and, if necessary, willingness to be the emotional punchbag), the more that they will assist the bereaved parent along the road which eventually leads to renewed independence and recovery.

6
Practical Necessities

These days, in developed countries where the health care is good, few young couples with a baby will have had any direct experience with death and will not be expecting to have to face such an experience at their age. When their baby does die suddenly and totally unexpectedly, they are pitched into a set of completely alien circumstances where they can feel very vulnerable indeed. At a time when they are least able to cope, they are asked to make decisions and arrangements which can have a very long-lasting affect. Many parents, rushed into such decisions, regret afterwards the actions which they took when they were in no fit state to think through the consequences. Because of this, I am setting out below a list of the practical necessities which tend to ensue after a cot death, to help newly bereaved couples to reach informed decisions and to help relatives, friends and professionals offer informed guidance to any newly bereaved couple known to them.

Coroner's officer

As mentioned in Chapter 2, a survey of 713 sudden infant deaths showed that 86 per cent occurred at home (or while visiting relatives or friends), 5.5 per cent in the car and 5 per cent in a public place, while only 3 per cent occurred on the way to hospital or within twenty-four hours of admission. Whatever the circumstances, when a much-loved baby is found dying or dead, the impact of chaos is immediate, yet in the midst of this chaos help needs to be summoned. Different families do this in a variety of ways, but the outcome is usually the same – parents find themselves encountering ambulance staff and a doctor at their home or medical staff at their nearest hospital, plus frequently the police and always the coroner's officer. He or she has a legal duty to investigate the baby's sudden and unexpected death and the first practical necessity after the death has been confirmed by a doctor is for the coroner's officer to be notified. This is usually done by one of the professionals in attendance, who should also explain clearly to the couple why the coroner's officer is being contacted and why someone in that position needs to be involved.

The coroner's officer who visited us arrived within half an hour of Elizabeth's death. His clipboard was very formal but his manner could not have been more gentle or kind, even when handling sensitive issues such as whether I would like to have her clothes returned to me at a later date. I can remember that reality intruded for an instant then, as I pictured all her clean clothes on the airing rack, waiting for her to wear them, but then shock resumed and cushioned me throughout the rest of the questioning.

Once the coroner's officer reports to the coroner, the usual next step is for the coroner to arrange for a post-mortem examination to be carried out by a pathologist. I don't know how other parents cope with the implications of this distressing necessity. I had to close my mind to what might have to be done to Elizabeth's body by telling myself that she was no longer a part of it and that her death might prevent other deaths by revealing vital clues. This was, I now realize, a naive hope since there are not many paediatric pathologists in this country – most post-mortems are carried out by general pathologists with time to do only a limited number of tests. Scotland fares better, for I have been told that there most babies *are* examined by paediatric pathologists and their reports are issued within 1–1½ hours afterwards.

Once the coroner receives the pathologist's and the coroner's officer's report, the coroner has discretion not to hold an inquest if he or she is satisfied that death was from natural causes. Inquests have become increasingly rare as the syndrome of SID has become more widely recognized.

Identification of the baby's body and seeing and holding the baby after death

Identification of the body is required if an inquest is to take place, but such identification is usually done formally before the baby's body is taken for autopsy and of course the decision as to whether to hold an inquest is usually only taken after the autopsy has been performed and other enquiries made. Some parents understandably see identification as an unnecessary and distressing procedure, which can involve them in delay and travel at a very vulnerable time. Thankfully the proportion of cases in which formal identification is requested seems to be declining (42 per cent in 1974–9, 36 per cent in 1980–1), but bereaved parents need to realize that such a

72

procedure may be one of the practical necessities imposed upon them.

Even if identification does not prove necessary, many parents may welcome the opportunity to see and hold their baby again, both as a means of expressing their love and as an aid to acknowledging the reality of what has happened. It is now well recognized that it is very important for parents to say goodbye. This does not mean that parents should feel obliged to see or hold the dead body of their baby if identification is not needed and the idea is too distressing, simply that the opportunity should be offered to them. In the survey covering the period of 1980–1, 77 per cent of parents expressed a wish to see and/or hold their baby again after death had been confirmed, yet 21 per cent were not given the opportunity to do so. For some, the experience can bring a sense of peace, but for others, especially if it is later and changes in appearance have been caused by the post-mortem examination, the experience can be a very upsetting one. Parents should be warned of any possible changes, but if they wish it they should be allowed easy access to their baby's body, either at the hospital or chapel of rest or at the mortuary or funeral parlour.

Donations for surgery

At the time of the baby's death the parents are usually too shocked and distraught to think about the possibility of donating any of the baby's organs to help others. Certainly this was true where Elizabeth was concerned and afterwards I felt guilty about it – perhaps other babies could have benefited and her death would not have seemed so totally in vain. I need not have worried. For transplant surgery to be successful, kidneys have to be removed within half an hour of death and eyes within six hours. In the case of an unexpected and undiagnosed death the law must take precedence; a post-mortem has to be carried out and this delay means that donation is not a practical possibility. Nor can the body be offered for medical teaching purposes, since it will not be accepted if a post-morten has taken place.

Photographs and keepsakes

These do not tend to be thought about during the immediate crisis, but their absence can cause distress at a later date. Most couples already have photos of their baby but, especially in the case of an older baby or child, these may not be current ones and whilst it may seem macabre to some to take photos of a baby or child who is already dead, I have known it to bring comfort to bereaved parents. Similarly with keepsakes such as a lock of hair, some couples may find the idea distressful whilst others may deeply regret not asking at the time. In both cases, the funeral director should be able to help and arrangements can be made at the chapel of rest, once the post-mortem has taken place and the baby has been laid out in readiness for the funeral. At such a time the baby is likely to have a more natural appearance than at the time immediately after death.

Suppression of milk

In less than five hours after their baby's death, mothers who have been breastfeeding are going to be only too uncomfortably aware that they have a plentiful supply of milk needing to be used and no baby to receive it. This presents a problem which is both a very practical and a very emotional one and advice is not always forthcoming or consistent. The best advice seems to be to take painkillers if necessary and to reduce fluid intake as much as possible for the first few days following the baby's death, leaving the breasts alone except to empty them once a day if an easy method is available (some mothers seem able to cope with portable breast pumps. I never succeeded when I needed to express milk and always found expressing by hand very much easier). In addition, some medical professionals still advise binding the breasts to encourage suppression of milk, with varying degrees of success. Some doctors are willing to prescribe medication such as Parladel or Estrovis to dry up the milk, but there are mixed views about whether it is wise to do so.

The pain caused by engorged breasts can be very severe and yet this is an aspect which does not seem to be given adequate attention by the medical profession. In May 1974, when our first daughter was born prematurely and died at birth, I was left with no baby but a plentiful supply of milk and the engorgement was very painful indeed. One nurse said: 'On no account must you express, you'll simply encourage more milk to come,' while another said: 'You must express to relieve the pressure, otherwise you'll get mastitis.' In the end I compromised with hot baths, letting the heat achieve the expressing for me, but it was a most upsetting experience.

When Elizabeth died, because I had been breastfeeding both babies I was in the fortunate position of still having a baby to receive my supply. The shock of Elizabeth's death reduced the supply in any case; Mary took as much as she needed and the rest I was able to express and store in small hospital bottles in a friend's freezer, just as I had done earlier when expressing my milk at home while the twins were still being tube-fed on the Special Care Unit. For mothers who wish to do so, it is well worth considering the possibility of donating excess milk to a milk bank for premature babies, since this can be a positive and rewarding action as well as a practical solution to the problem.

Sadly the reality of the milk reinforces the loss of the baby. It was my wise sister who observed: 'I bet everyone's saying how lucky you are to have had twins, but I won't because I know that having one won't reduce the grief of losing the other at all.' She was right, of course, but at least Mary was there to hug. I know that when our first baby died I used to move carefully in my sleep, thinking that she was still safely inside me, only to jerk awake to the realization of my new and unexpected flatness. Then I would lie in the dark, aching to hold the baby who wasn't there. That same aching occurred after Elizabeth's death but thankfully Mary was there to give and receive the cuddles we both needed so much, though I never deluded myself into thinking that she was anyone other than her own lovely self.

Retrieval of the baby's clothes or bedding

Some decisions have to be made very quickly after the baby has died and one of them is whether you wish to retrieve clothes and bedding after their removal for examination. Some parents will not wish to be reminded of their baby in this way but for others, such associations with the baby can be very precious and unless they state their wishes at the time, the clothes and bedding may simply be discarded and later destroyed. It is helpful if officials associated with the baby's death – the police, the coroner's officer, the funeral director – can take the time to raise the subject of keepsakes and clothing, since the parents may well be too shocked to think of such matters until it is too late.

The baby's possessions

The same is true where possessions of the baby are concerned.

During the period of shock, parents may make very hasty decisions such as removing everything connected with their baby – cot, pram, carrycot, buggy, clothes, toys etc. This may seem sensible at the time, since every association is so painful, but later some parents may come to regret the fact that they have no reminders, no special toy to keep. Such symbols of love become helpful because they can allow us to talk about the baby who has died. Items such as the cot or pram may seem 'infected' or 'jinxed' in some way at the time and parents may vow never to use them again, but strangely enough using the same cot, carrycot, pram or buggy for a subsequent baby can be a very effective way of overcoming fears and increasing parental confidence.

Port-mortem findings and registered cause of death

Because they feel so bewildered at the unexpected death of their baby or child, parents need to hear the post-mortem findings and registerable cause of death as soon as possible. They should be told; they should not have to ask. In the 1974–81 survey, between 55 and 60 per cent were informed by the coroner or coroner's officer or police; only 12 per cent were informed by their GP; nearly 10 per cent learned of the cause of death from the registrar of deaths; some learned from the undertaker and one family learned from the local newspaper, surely an unforgiveable occurrence. As many as 40 per cent of parents said that they were given no explanation of the post-mortem findings or the cause of death by a medically qualified person, so obviously this is an area where GPs or paediatricians could do more to help in the future.

It is very important that parents should be told in advance of the procedure and arrangements for informing them of the cause of death, otherwise they are left in unbearable limbo. There should be no undue delay in carrying out the post-mortem examination as this only increases the distress of the parents and reduces the chances of evidence being found which might explain the death. Obviously microscopic findings may take weeks to become available, but there should be no delay in informing parents of the initial results. Parents in England and Wales are entitled under the 1984 Coroner's Rules to be shown a copy of the post-mortem report, either directly or via their GP (because of the medical terminology involved, it is usually helpful to study the report together with the GP or paediatrician) and as parents you should not hesitate to exercise this right.

Registering the death

The 1953 Births and Deaths Registration Act requires that, except when an inquest is held, the death has to be registered by personal attendance of a 'qualified informant' within five days of death (this period can be extended to fourteen days if the informant sends written notice to the registrar within the five days that the Medical Certificate of Cause of Death has been signed by a doctor). To register the death, the registrar needs either a Certificate after Inquest from the coroner or a Pink Form A or B, depending on the circumstances.

Having to register their baby's death in the same place where they only recently registered the birth is an unavoidable but harrowing experience for many parents, especially as other babies are frequently present while they are waiting. In our case it became bizarre because one of the officials, seeing us with Mary on our knee, said: 'Oh, how lovely – you've come to register her birth, have you?' Go together if you possibly can, to support each other, because the finality of registration is very difficult to bear. I can remember that when we left the registrar's office we wandered aimlessly round the nearest shop for nearly half an hour, simply trying to regain some grasp on reality.

Financial assistance

When Elizabeth died there was a death grant available, but it was only £9, a pathetically small amount. We found the receipt of it very distressing, for it seemed to imply that that was all Elizabeth was considered to be worth. We donated it to the FSID for we wanted nothing to do with it. Since then the death grant has been abolished, but families in receipt of Income Support may be able to receive financial assistance towards the costs of the funeral. As the amount would vary according to family circumstances, it would be necessary to contact your local DSS office in order to obtain further details and in order to apply. There are leaflets available concerning Income Support and also concerning what to do after a death and it is worth obtaining copies, for accurate information.

Funeral arrangements

When a baby dies suddenly and the death is referred to the coroner, either his officer or the police arrange, at the coroner's expense, for an undertaker to remove the body from the place of death to a mortuary for a post-mortem examination by a pathologist of the coroner's choice. As with ambulance staff, how the initial funeral director handles the baby's body is of great importance to the parents and deep distress is known to have been caused when the director has simply bundled the body into a case for removal, instead of handling the baby in a compassionate and sensitive manner. Parents do not need to use the same undertaker for the actual funeral and indeed, in the 1974–9 survey, 97 per cent chose not to do so. In this same survey 18 per cent chose their own undertaker via a list given to them by the police or coroner's officer; 21 per cent took the advice of family or friends and 12 per cent used a firm already known to the family; 12 per cent took the advice of their minister of religion, 10 per cent chose the nearest firm and 7 per cent the only one in the district. In 4 per cent it was the grandparents who chose the undertaker and paid for the funeral arrangements. In 1 per cent the DSS arranged and paid; 3 per cent chose funeral directors on the advice of health professionals such as their doctor or health visitor and the remainder chose from advertisements.

Over half of the parents received neither an estimate of the cost of the funeral nor an explanation of the costs incurred, a disturbing proportion in view of the high costs entailed. If you can cope yourself or you can enlist someone to act on your behalf, then it is worth contacting a number of funeral directors and obtaining quotations before choosing. The funeral director who came to us was kind and efficient and took total control of the arrangements. It was just as well, for the world into which I had retreated at the time was so private that very little penetrated.

At an emotional and difficult time the bereaved parents have to make an early decision as to whether they wish their baby to be buried or cremated. This is necessary in order for the coroner to issue the correct certificates. It is very easy at such a vulnerable time to simply accede to the wishes of a partner or relatives without thinking through the implications. Some parents who chose cremation have been known to later regret their decision when they realized that there would never be a grave for them to visit as a focal point for their mourning. As The Revd Ron Robinson sagely pointed out during a talk which he gave on bereavement in April 1989, graves make excellent muttering spots, somewhere for parents to feel at liberty to say and do things which they would not otherwise be allowed to do. After a cremation, if there are any ashes these can be interned, thereby providing a place to mourn, or they may be scattered in a Garden of Remembrance. Whilst parents are welcome to visit such gardens, they do not offer the focal point provided by a grave.

The question of ashes is a vexed one, for there has been inconsistency in the past, with some funeral directors insisting that no ashes remain when a baby dies under the age of 6 months, whilst others maintain that, with care and special procedures (waiting until the end of the day, allowing the heat of the furnace to drop and putting the remains through only one filter instead of two), it is possible to salvage some residue if the parents so wish. Since parents often need somewhere which they can identify as their baby's 'resting-place' as part of their grieving, the issue is an important one and great distress can be caused if parents who were told that no ashes would remain meet parents who have been given ashes for internment. Following representations made to the Home Office by the FSID and others, a new Regulation 23 has been introduced which requires that the cremation authority informs applicants when it appears that cremation may not result in identifiable ashes, thus allowing the parents to withdraw or continue in the knowledge that there may be no ashes. It is hoped that, as a result, a consistent policy may emerge in the future, to prevent unnecessary distress to bereaved families.

Funerals are very expensive. A cremation has the advantage of being less expensive than a burial and for many couples, the thought of the cleansing effect of fire is preferable to that of their baby's body being placed in the ground and covered with earth. I have heard of mothers distraught with grief at such a moment, throwing themselves on to the tiny coffin in an instinctive bid to protect their small baby, and a number of mothers have told me of their urge to go back afterwards and lay a blanket over the grave to keep their baby warm, just as they would have done in life. Our natural parental responses do not cease when our baby dies and the urge to cuddle and to protect is a very basic and strong one which fights for recognition long after the baby has died. I can remember that I dreaded seeing the coffin because I knew how pathetically small it would look, but the reality proved to be less distressing than I had expected. The coffin *was* very small, but it was also very clean and white and neat, complete in itself and somehow restful-looking.

If the parents cannot in any way afford the costs of the funeral, and if no grants or other forms of financial assistance are forth-coming, they may need to request a simple disposal – burial in a communal grave in their absence, with no mourners, cars, or church service and only a very basic wooden coffin. Such a solution is unlikely to answer their needs, for the ritual of the funeral service often plays a very important part in the process of grieving. It allows the family to acknowledge the reality of what has happened and to say goodbye to their baby and it provides a focal point and permissible outlet for their grief and that of their friends and relatives.

After Elizabeth's funeral service, family and friends gave support by coming to our house. Some of our friends accompanied us to the funeral, but two friends stayed behind – one to prepare all the food and another to look after Rebecca and Mary. Within my private world I was nevertheless very aware of just how fortunate we were in having such good friends and of how much their support meant to us. The shock waves of Elizabeth's death had rippled right through our community and I knew that many friends and neighbours were grieving with us as well as for us, that the loss was theirs, too.

The funeral of a baby is harrowing both for the families and friends and for the ministers involved and can call into question the faith in God of all concerned. The minister has an unenviable task to perform and is often deeply affected. Like the doctor or health visitor, he can feel very helpless and inadequate in the face of such tragedy, but his presence and his carefully chosen words and service can be of immense comfort to bereaved families.

Where the parents do not have any religious beliefs, or do not want a church service, then it is sometimes possible to arrange a special non-religious service at their home. Perhaps Australia has the right idea, for there it is possible to ask a civil celebrant to conduct the ceremony for burial on a non-religious basis. Whatever funeral arrangements are chosen, bereaved parents should be encouraged to take an active part in the decision-making process, since they need to experience the pain involved if later recovery is to be successfully achieved.

Medical records

One of the useful functions which the health visitor can perform is to ensure that medical records are altered as soon as possible, otherwise parents may find themselves facing the very upsetting experience of receiving an appointment for a child or baby who is already dead. The health visitor will usually undertake to cancel any appointments and to notify the Family Practitioner Committee, hospital and Child Health Clinic, but it makes sense for parents to check that this is being done on their behalf.

Financial arrangements

Child benefit

When your child dies, you should not cash any order after the date of death and you should return your Child Benefit Book to the DSS for alteration. I well remember the simple but brutal line which was drawn through Elizabeth's name, retaining the names of Rebecca and Mary in the same book and merely overstamping the weekly amounts. Since that time the DSS has given instructions that a new book should always be issued, with temporary giros to cover unexpired but valid payments from the old book, so if you do have older children, it is worth asking for a new book to be issued when you submit the one relating to the baby who has died.

Savings accounts

Any such accounts will need to be closed. It is also in your own interest to cash any Premium Bonds which may have been bought on your child's behalf. The form-filling involved is an added stress, but preferable to the slight risk of receiving a prize-winning notification addressed to a child who has been dead for some time.

Free dental treatment and free prescriptions

As mothers you are entitled to free dental treatment and free prescriptions for a year following your baby's birth, so do not let yourself be told otherwise – they are yours as a right and you should claim them.

Coping with the Press

Making an announcement

Many parents, especially if they announced their baby's birth, also like to announce his or her sudden and unexpected death. This can help to reduce the number of painful occasions when enquiries are made about the baby's progress by those unaware that death has occurred. There are inherent dangers, however, of which parents should be aware. We were warned by our funeral director that placing such an announcement might 'attract the wrong sort of people'. For the same reason, he advised us to have the coffin lid sealed beforehand and I can remember the shock of realizing that there really could be strangers who would wish to intrude upon our grief in such a way.

Notification of the Press

Apparently the police are obliged to inform the Press of any death if they are asked to do so, but they do try and encourage the Press not to pester bereaved parents. In the 1974–81 survey, 5 per cent of parents complained about sensationalized or inaccurate reports of their child's death, published without their prior knowledge or permission. Many parents were distressed by misleading descriptions of the cause of death and the fact that, via the police, the Press had learned the cause of death before the parents themselves had been told. Lawfully the Press may only report a post-mortem finding if the coroner has authorized it. The Coroner's Rules 1984 (S.1.552), Rule 10(2) states: 'Unless authorized by the coroner, the person making a post-mortem examination shall not supply a copy of his report to any person other than the coroner.'

Reports in the media

As awareness of cot deaths has increased, so the rate of reportage in the media has increased as well. Some reports have been misleading or inaccurate, causing great distress to bereaved families. As cot-death parents we are very vulnerable when inaccurate theories or reports are published, so it is worth heeding the advice given by the FSID in their August 1984 *Newsletter* (adapted from advice issued by Dr John Maloney, Monash University, and reprinted by courtesy of the SID Research Foundation, Australia):

> *How to evaluate media reports on 'cot death'*
> *Ignore the headlines* – often they do not accurately describe the article/contents.
> *Read the text and underline the words* 'might', 'may', 'possibly', 'could' . . . This helps to emphasize any uncertainties in the report.
> *Re-read* the text – then ask yourself these questions:
>
> (i) *Are the deaths sudden, unexpected, and without adequate*

explanation? Is the report consistent with the definition of SIDS or *are the deaths sudden but explained deaths*?

(ii) *Does it take into account that sudden unexplained infant deaths occurred in earlier centuries and that the rate has changed little over the years*? This means that suggested theories relating to modern technology or recent changes in child-care practice are unlikely to hold the key or provide the clue to the majority of unexplained deaths.

(iii) *Is the article based on an idea that has not yet been tested*? Have experiments not yet been performed?

(iv) *Is the article a report of a random observation*? Have they seen only one or just a few cases? Does it need further work to establish a hypothesis?

Remember

(a) The scientist may not have said what is reported.

(b) The need for over-simplification may lead to the wrong impression.

(c) The interest of the scientist may have been in another area. It may have been the journalist who asked about a possible relationship to cot death which led to it becoming a headline.

Although the periodic occurrence of banner headlines can cause unnecessary and untold distress to bereaved families, at least the heightened publicity surrounding cot death means that many more people are aware of the syndrome and thankfully they are usually sensible enough to see through accusative theories for which there is no evidence and to treat them with the contempt they deserve. I had agreed to do a street collection for cot death shortly after one such unproven theory exploded across the front pages of the newspapers. I had feared a hostile reception from the public but instead received understanding, interest and a willingness to contribute generously to the research which is trying to find the answers. Such generosity not only helps the research, it demonstrates tangibly that other people do feel compassion for families bereaved by a cot death.

7
Helpers

The reason why the whole of an earlier chapter was devoted to family and friends was because firstly, they also suffer badly when a baby or child known to them dies suddenly in a cot death and secondly, they can contribute so much to the bereaved family, helping on both a practical and an emotional level. In the 1974–81 survey of 713 unexpected infant deaths, 72 per cent of parents claimed that relatives were amongst the most helpful, with 55 per cent naming close friends as being the next most valuable. Any summary of those who can help must start, therefore, by emphasizing family and friends, the people who knew your baby and with whom you will be able to share very special and valuable memories. Other sources of help are also available, however, and they are therefore listed below, in the hope that bereaved families will be able to benefit from their existence.

Support groups

Bereaved parents have told me that, apart from family and close friends, of all the possible sources of help available, meeting other parents who have suffered a cot death often proves to be the most valuable. Attending a group meeting is in some ways easier than arranging to meet on a one-to-one basis, since parents who simply wish to sit and listen can do so without any pressure on them to talk of their experiences or feelings unless they choose to do so. Those attending group meetings tend to vary greatly in the length of time since their babies died, from very newly bereaved to those who have had a number of years in which to try to come to terms with their loss, and this can be very helpful. Newly bereaved parents are able to identify with others in a similar situation to themselves but they are also able to see that it is possible not merely to survive a cot death but in many ways to recover and grow.

As there was no local Friends of the Foundation support group in my area at the time, I did not attend a support-group meeting until I moved to a different part of the country, three years after Elizabeth's death. I found it very strange to walk into a room full of parents who had experienced a similar loss and grief. I did not know what to expect and was amazed to find everyone so outgoing and cheerful. Beneath this ability to still enjoy life, I could sense an automatic bond, one which made the usual need for polite small-talk totally redundant. In her very moving article, 'Thoughts of a mother', Carolyn Czybist wrote of the time when, three years after the death of her baby son, she received a list of other cot-death parents and telephoned fourteen of them in one week. She found that being able to talk to others like herself released 'so many locked up feelings . . . It was a strange blend of hearing other people say what I had been feeling, and feeling along with them what I was hearing them say. When we all finally met as a group, it can only be described as a warm reunion of very old friends; there were no strangers.'

I would certainly recommend support groups to anyone who has experienced a cot death, not just for the months immediately following the death but also at future times, especially for support during the months and first year following a subsequent pregnancy and birth. If, however, the thought of facing a room full of people is too daunting, many local groups have individual mothers and fathers who are very willing to visit bereaved families in the safe privacy of their own homes and this can be a good source of help for those who do not yet feel ready to cope in company. Whilst there is always a risk of finding that you and the befriender have nothing in common other than your shared experience, there is also a good chance that you will find great support and as a result of sharing such deep personal feelings, close and lasting friendships can often result. Most areas now have local groups and the address and telephone number of the nearest should be available at your doctor's surgery, the coroner's or registrar's office or the local library or Citizens' Advice Bureau. If it is not, a list is kept by the FSID and they are always willing to put parents in touch with the local contact.

Compassionate Friends and TAMBA

As well as the FSID support groups, other valuable self-help groups also exist and these may be especially useful to parents in particular situations, such as those who lose an older child in a cot death (the Compassionate Friends organization exists to help bereaved parents of children of all ages) and those who lose a twin or triplet (TAMBA, the Twins and Multiple Births Association, exists to support families of such children). In the case of TAMBA, many parents may already have had contact following the birth of their twins or triplets, for advice and support on how to cope. This support does not need to end if one of the babies or children dies, for parents of other twins often have special insight into what bereaved parents may be suffering and TAMBA may be able to introduce bereaved parents to others who have suffered a similar loss. A leaflet exists entitled: *The Cot Death of your Twin Baby* and this is available from TAMBA, at a minimal price.

Fundraising and befriending

A cot death can leave an overwhelming sense of helplessness. One way to overcome this is by giving time and effort to fundraising. This is primarily an active, physical commitment rather than an emotional one and can therefore be easier to handle in the months following your baby's death. You will need to feel emotionally strong enough to cope with members of the public who may unwittingly make hurtful remarks. Standing on a street corner rattling a tin will not benefit you if every refusal to donate feels like a personal rejection, but if you can cope with these aspects, fundraising can be very useful and there is the tangible result of money raised by you which can then be forwarded for research projects. Some parents are excellent at persuading the public to donate, others have a flair for coffee mornings, jumble sales, sponsored activities or more unusual fundraising events, and all are equally valid (provided that they are legal!). It is a very positive way of saying to your baby: 'I don't know why you died, but I'm going to do all I can to help finance those who may be able to find out the answers and perhaps in time they will be able to prevent other babies like you from dying as well.'

Fundraising activities are easier if done as a group. If no local group exists, it is worth considering the possibility of becoming a local contact yourself and establishing a group, either to befriend, or to fundraise, or both. No special skills are needed for befriending, just an ability to listen and to share. To help others, you will need to feel that you have sufficiently come to terms with your own grief and are back on an even emotional keel and this usually takes at least a year from the time of your baby's death.

Befriending can be a big commitment, since having offered support you will need to be able to continue giving it for as long as it is required. Realistically, this means that normally you will need the support of your own partner and family, since unexpected telephone calls or urgent requests for a visit can sometimes disrupt existing family plans. As you may meet cot-death parents from widely differing backgrounds and cultures, you will have to be a tolerant person who feels no desire to try and impose one particular set of beliefs or views on anyone else and you will have to be sensitive and observant enough to know when to refer families to some form of professional help if befriending is not enough to solve their problems or answer their needs. It would be important not to get involved in medical or legal matters and it would be necessary to keep up to date with accurate information via the FSID. Having said all that and having made befriending sound a daunting prospect, it can be of tremendous help both to those whom you befriend and also to you yourself. The FSID has prepared a leaflet called *Guidelines for Befrienders*, and this is available free from their office in London. The FSID also organizes training sessions for anyone interested in offering support to others. It hopes to increase the number of such sessions in the future, to ensure that volunteers are well informed and prepared beforehand and that a consistent policy prevails.

Videos and books

It may seem morbid or even voyeuristic to want to learn the details of other cot deaths and witness the grief of other families, but there is something very comforting indeed in the recognition of shared experiences and emotions. In this respect, there are videos available which might prove helpful (details of these are given in Appendix 1). Even the title of one of the videos – *My Beautiful Baby is Dead* – brought me close to tears when I first saw it and I found the sense of shared grief helpful. This particular video showed the work of the Hampshire Parent Support Group. Other videos are also available and they can be hired from the FSID (a minimal charge is made to cover outgoing postage and packing, plus the cost of paying the return registered postage). If used by groups of parents, they can provide a useful focus and starting point for discussion of worries or problems. If used by parents in their own home, they can bring comfort and a recognition of what one of the other titles says: *You Are Not Alone*.

As well as the videos, at the time of writing I am aware of four other books on the subject of cot death and these, too, can prove very helpful (for details, see Appendix 1).

FSID (Foundation for the Study of Infant Deaths)

I would urge all bereaved families to contact the Foundation, not because I want to increase their workload but simply because they are the most informed counselling service available and they can give details of local contacts who may be able to help. As mentioned in Chapter 2, the Foundation is a registered charity which was formed in 1971 with three main aims:

- to raise funds for research into the causes and prevention of cot death
- to support bereaved families
- to act as a centre for information about cot death

Over the years the Foundation has raised millions of pounds for research, held numerous Study Days for parents and professionals, established a network of support throughout the country and worked hard to make its existence known to doctors, coroners, funeral directors, the police and hospital staff, so that newly bereaved parents are not left in isolation with no information or support available. But it has been an uphill struggle.

When Elizabeth died in September 1979, *no one* was able to give us any information at all. Since there had to be a reason for her death, I tried to convince myself that she must have suffocated because of the position in which I'd found her. For over four months Pat and I lived in a kind of limbo, until in desperation I wrote to a magazine asking if there was any organization that could tell me anything at all about cot deaths. The magazine sent me the address of the FSID and I summoned up enough courage to write. Their response was exactly what I had needed. All my questions were answered clearly and sensitively, my layman's theories treated tactfully and with respect. Although they handle thousands of letters from bereaved parents, they made me feel individual and special and I felt that they could genuinely understand some of what I was experiencing at the time. Had we known of their existence when Elizabeth died, we would not have felt so totally alone. Thankfully the situation has improved since then. The FSID is more widely known and, hopefully, the more information that is available, the more chance there is that such situations will be avoided in the future.

Ambulance crew and hospital staff

When both the doctor and an ambulance are summoned to a baby who does not seem to be breathing, it is the ambulance staff who are very often the first to arrive on the scene and their response and actions can have a critical affect on the shocked and distraught parents. Ambulance and hospital staff are professionals and parents recognize this but as a result they tend to have high expectations, hoping that some magical action on the part of the professionals will restore their baby to life. It may be very obvious to the professionals that the baby is already dead and that there is nothing that they can do, but it is worth bearing in mind that any attempt at resuscitation, no matter how hopeless, may bring peace of mind to the distressed parents in the future, a reassurance that everything possible was done to save their baby. If resuscitation is clearly not appropriate, the use of a stethoscope can help parents to realize that death has indeed occurred.

How ambulance and hospital staff handle the baby is of vital importance. Gentle and sensitive handling is essential and the baby should always be treated as one would treat a live, healthy baby, even if death has already taken place. If this is the case, it can help if the staff can wrap the baby protectively in a shawl or blanket and hand him or her to the parents for a last, crucial cuddle if the parents so wish. Again, the staff must be sensitive to the parents' needs at a time when they may be too deeply shocked to express their own wishes.

Although there are rules concerning carrying dead bodies or allowing one or other of the parents to accompany the baby to hospital, ambulance staff should if at all possible be flexible about such regulations and place the needs of the parents above the needs of the rule book.

Even though the baby may be dead and the ambulance staff therefore technically redundant, parents will appreciate their reassuring and coping presence and it helps in such cases if the staff can give some time to the parents and at least wait until the doctor, coroner's officer or another supportive adult arrives to take their place.

It is easier for staff if there is any sign of life in the baby, for then they have a positive role to play and can undertake immediate resuscitation procedures. It is not just the parents who feel totally helpless if the baby is already dead. Ambulance and emergency staff are members of families, too, and feel not only the despair of the parents but also their own grief at witnessing such a tragedy and being unable to restore the baby to life. As professionals, they have to remain in control of the situation, but they should not feel that they must hide their emotion. It can be very helpful to parents to see that others, too, are affected by their baby's death. I am still grateful to the ambulanceman who showed me, through his tears, that he cared as well.

Ambulance and hospital staff are used to coping with death and tragedy, but that does not make them immune to the affects and it can help the staff if they are given the opportunity to talk about their feelings with work colleagues or an independent listener. It is easy to forget that professionals have needs. They carry an immense emotional burden and if they are not given the opportunity to share the load there is a risk that in time it will become too heavy to bear. One of the actions which local cot-death support groups can undertake is to invite ambulance and hospital staff to one of their meetings. Staff who only ever witness the total shock and despair of suddenly bereaved parents can find it helpful to meet similar parents at a future date and to see for themselves that parents do survive and cope and that recovery and even happiness do become possible.

Accident and emergency staff need to be well informed about cot death in order to be able to cope and to help bereaved parents. Sudden death in infancy, therefore, should feature as part of their training. If it does not do so already, it would be useful for staff to ask for such training to be made available. No one should be expected to cope with such a traumatic situation without being fully prepared beforehand. Because staff have such a crucial role to play, the FSID has issued a set of guidelines to help them, as follows:

Sequence of action in accident and emergency department

Infant arrives moribund or dead

(1) Verification of death should be made in the Accident Department rather than in the ambulance.
(2) If resuscitation is attempted or while the baby's condition is being evaluated, a brief history of the baby's health and recent events should be taken from an accompanying parent.

(3) Every effort should be made to provide a room or privacy for the distressed parents.

(4) Ensure that a suitable person is looking after the baby's brothers and sisters who may have come with the parent(s).

(5) If only one parent is present, and agrees, contact the other parent or relative.

(6) INFORM (i) a member of the paediatric department.

(7) INFORM (ii) the hospital chaplain, if parents request a dying child to be baptized or wish for his support.

(8) Review information briefly before breaking the news that the baby is dead. Parents will need privacy in which to express their grief.

(9) After an appropriate interval, inform parents of the need for a post-mortem examination to establish the cause of death, which will be arranged by the coroner.

(10) Unless there is a history of diagnosed illness, obvious signs of injury, or the parental attitude arouses suspicion, explain to the parents that the death appears to be a cot death (also called sudden infant death syndrome).

(11) Explain to parents that it is the coroner's duty to investigate all sudden deaths of unknown cause and that they will be asked to make a statement to the coroner's officer or police, who may visit their homes and may take the baby's bedding for examination to help establish the cause of death. This does not mean that anybody will be blamed or that an inquest will necessarily be held.

(12) INFORM (iii) the hospital Social Work Department. Someone should remain with the parents until they leave.

(13) INFORM (iv) the coroner's officer and explain whether death appears to be natural or unnatural.

(14) Offer parents an opportunity to see their baby and let them hold her or him before the baby is taken to the mortuary. The infant should be clothed and made as presentable as possible.

(15) If identification of the body to the coroner's officer or police is required, a member of staff or hospital chaplain should accompany the parents to the mortuary.

(16) Offer parents copies of the leaflet *Information for Parents following the Sudden and Unexpected Death of their Baby*, which gives the address and telephone number of the Foundation for the Study of Infant Deaths.

(17) Discuss with the parents arrangements for continued support.

(18) INFORM (v) the family doctor
           (vi) the health visitor
           (vii) the social worker, if already involved with the family.

(19) The mother, if breastfeeding, will need immediate advice on suppression of lactation.

(20) Ensure that the parents have suitable transport to take them home.

The doctor and the health visitor

Much of what has been said about ambulance and hospital emergency staff applies to doctors as well. They are often the first on the scene, and the family tends to have high expectations that the doctor can perform a miracle and restore their baby to life. The doctor may well have to cope with the family's feelings of disillusionment and anger if this proves not to be the case. Like the ambulance crew, the doctor needs to handle the baby in a sensitive manner, undertake any action which may help the baby or the parents and, whilst remaining professional, not be afraid to show that he cares and is affected by the baby's death.

Because the parents will be in shock, the doctor will need to explain the situation very clearly to them and probably give details more than once as the parents may be unable to comprehend what is being said to them. They need to be told kindly but firmly if death has already taken place, so that they can begin to accept the reality of what has happened. To avoid the damaging effects of guilt, they also need the doctor's reassurance that the death appears to be a cot death and that at present cot deaths can neither be predicted nor prevented.

Even if the GP is not present at the time of the baby's death, he or she should contact the parents as quickly as possible afterwards in order to offer support. Following a cot death, GPs have a very important role to play on both a practical and an emotional level. As soon as details are available, they should ensure that the parents are given an explanation of the post-mortem findings and the registered cause of death and they should make themselves available to the family, preferably via a home visit. Although a doctor does not have a legal duty to attend a baby who is obviously dead, failure to help the family at such a time can cause deep distress and may permanently destroy the doctor/patient relationship. When given, the doctor's presence and support are much appreciated.

Because the doctor's role is so important, the FSID has issued guidelines and these are reproduced in an adapted form below:

Check list – GP support for the family

(1) As soon as you hear of the baby's death, contact the family to express sympathy, by a home visit if possible. Early support prevents later misunderstandings.

(2) Unless there is obvious injury, a history of illness or the parental attitude arouses suspicion, tell the parents it appears to be a cot death but that a post-mortem examination will be necessary to establish the cause of death. If death remains unexplained, it may be registered as sudden infant death syndrome. Some parents want to see or hold their child after death is confirmed but before the body is taken to a mortuary.

(3) Explain the coroner's duty, the possibility of an inquest, and warn parents that they or relatives may be asked to identify the body. Advise the parents that they will be asked to make a statement to the coroner's officer or police, and that bedding may be taken for examination to help establish the cause of death. If necessary, give advice on registering the death and making funeral arrangements. The coroner's officer may need to know parents' choice of burial or cremation.

(4) If considering offering parents a drug to alleviate the initial shock, it is known that many do not want anxiolytics or anti-depressants, but prefer something to induce sleep.

(5) If the mother was breastfeeding, give advice on suppression of lactation; prescribe medication and advise her to leave the breasts alone except to empty them once a day if an easy method is available.

(6) Take particular note of siblings. Remember that twin babies carry extra risk of cot death and that a surviving twin may need hospitalization for observation. Give guidance on emotional needs of siblings, who may be neglected or over-protected; reassure parents that older children are not at risk.

(7) Advise parents of likely grief reactions such as aching arms, hearing the baby cry, distressing dreams, and strong positive or negative sexual feelings, but reassure them that these and other symptoms such as loss of appetite and sleeplessness are normal and temporary. Anger, sometimes directed towards the GP, guilt and self-blame, especially on the part of the

mother, are common grief reactions for which the doctor should be prepared.

(8) Offer parents copies of the Foundation's *Information for Parents* leaflet.

(9) Make sure that parents have a relative or close friend very near them during the forty-eight hours after the death, and offer explanation to them and to the minister of religion. Make sure the family's health visitor and other members of the primary care team know of the baby's death and are prepared to give continued support.

(10) Arrange a subsequent meeting with the parents to discuss the cause of death. Make sure the coroner informs you of the initial and final post-mortem findings and consult with the pathologist if any clarification is needed.

(11) Offer parents a later interview with a paediatrician, both for themselves and the siblings. An independent opinion is mutually beneficial to the parents and GP, restoring parental confidence in the primary care team and sharing some of the load of counselling, particularly concerning future children.

(12) Parents who have lost a baby unexpectedly will need extra attention and support with their subsequent children from their obstetrician, paediatrician, general practitioner and health visitor.

I gather that a group practice of two or three doctors is likely to have a cot death every three to five years and that a single doctor with an average-sized practice may encounter a cot death only once every eight years. Thankfully that's not often, but it means, of course, that the doctor and his or her health visitors may feel almost as helpless and bewildered as the parents themselves. The FSID has given much time and effort to circularizing surgeries with all the appropriate literature but inevitably there are still surgeries where no leaflets are available and where the medical staff may feel at a loss to help.

We belonged to a group practice when Elizabeth died and it was one of the other partners who came and certified that she was dead. He left within minutes of doing so, after an unhelpful: 'I'm sorry, it's one of those things.' I never saw my own doctor. My health visitor's reaction was genuine distress but a helpless: 'I'm sorry, I know nothing about cot death. I don't understand why it happens and there's nothing any of us can do.' When I asked how much Mary might be at risk her reply was: 'No, no, dear, lightning never strikes twice.' Lightning *can* strike again in the same place on different occasions and I don't regret our round-the-clock surveillance in the weeks and months that followed, because I know now that, being a twin, Mary *was* at increased risk. Where the health visitors are interested and well informed, their support can be invaluable, yet in the 1974–81 survey of 713 unexpected infant deaths 17 per cent of parents had no contact with their health visitor or midwife at all after their baby's death and felt very abandoned.

The information is available. By encouraging doctors and health visitors to seek out the relevant information and offer support, parents will also be helping future cot-death parents as well as assisting the doctors and health visitors themselves, since fore-warned is forearmed. Most doctors and health visitors want to do all they can to help but if they are not conversant with the literature that exists, they can feel at a loss to do so. They are in a very difficult position. Their role is usually an active and practical one, 'making things better'. Suddenly they are faced with a situation which can't be made better; the baby is dead and no one can alter that tragic reality. Many health visitors who have to cope with a cot death experience shock, grief, soul-searching and a strong element of self-flagellation. If a cot death happens more than once in their career, this can undermine their faith in their own abilities and make them feel like a Jonah.

Coping with the sudden death of a baby is very different to coping with a sick baby or child and, like the parents, health visitors are hampered by the fact that there is no warning and therefore no time to prepare for the event. There are, however, positive ways in which they can be of help, such as ensuring that all clinic appointments for the deceased child are cancelled immediately and that the Family Practitioner Committee, hospital and Child Health Clinic are all informed, to avoid the distress caused if parents are sent a future appointment for a child who is already dead. This is a useful course of action, but being unable to give the parents a reason for the child's death can make health visitors feel very helpless. There is also a tendency for the parents' anxiety over any subsequent baby to transfer itself to the health visitor, causing worry over every little symptom which would never even have been considered before the experience of a cot death. At such times it can be helpful for both health visitors and parents to seek reassurance by referring to the FSID guidelines about when to consult a doctor about the baby (see Appendix 3).

Being professionals, health visitors feel obliged to project a confidence and reassurance which they may not themselves be feeling, and they can find their visits very draining emotionally, but these visits are often of enormous help to bereaved families.

As a figure of authority, sensitive and appropriate words from the health visitor at the time of the baby's death can bring immense comfort. Insensitive or inappropriate words can cause immense distress. When parents are in deep shock, it is easy for them to mishear or misunderstand and similarly it is very difficult for them to absorb what is being said, so like doctors, health visitors will need to express themselves very carefully and may need to repeat factual information a number of times for it to be accepted and understood. New information about cot death is constantly being discovered and with so many demands upon their time it is difficult for health professionals to keep up to date, but the more informed they can become on the subject, the more they will be able to help newly bereaved families.

Paediatrician

The paediatrician sometimes is more likely to possess a specialized knowledge about cot death than a general practitioner, but at one time he or she was unlikely to be involved except in response to a specific request from the family. In the survey of 713 unexpected infant deaths, only 8 per cent of parents mentioned seeing a paediatrician following their baby's death, but of those who did, 59 per cent indicated that the paediatrician was among those who gave greatest support. Fortunately since the time of the survey it has been decided that a consultant paediatrician should be designated in each health district to take a special interest in sudden death in infancy –the FSID will probably be able to tell you if one exists in your area, although you might have to make your own arrangements to meet (usually via your own doctor).

Since the launch of the CONI scheme (Care of the Next Infant, see Chapter 8, pp. 110-13) the situation has continued to improve. It is hoped that, in time, every cot-death family will be offered the chance to meet the appropriate paediatrician in their area so that they can ask any questions which may be worrying them and so that they can obtain information and advice. The paediatrician can do much to reassure families that, at the present state of knowledge, cot death is neither predictable nor preventable and that they are therefore in no way to blame. Coming from someone in authority, such reassurance is welcome and helpful. A number of paediatricians do now take an active interest in the sudden infant death syndrome and are of immense support to bereaved families. It is hoped that, in the future, the situation will continue to improve, as a well-informed and interested paediatrician can do so much to allay fears and guilt and to answer questions about the syndrome.

The police and the coroner's officer

It may seem strange to some parents to include police under the heading *Helpers*, because they can seem to be simply an added stress at an already extremely stressful time, but it is worth realizing that they can also be a source of strength and reassurance, a confirmation that no one has been to blame.

Police involvement is a legal requirement in England and Wales when a sudden and unexpected death occurs (in Scotland sudden deaths are investigated by the Procurator-fiscal). The coroner is obliged by law to inquire into such deaths and usually this is done on the coroner's behalf by a coroner's officer. The majority of coroner's officers are serving police officers seconded to assist the coroner. In many areas of the country, especially rural ones, the coroner's officer arranges for the local police to make the initial investigation. What often happens is that the police are called to the scene before the coroner's officer, sometimes by parents or neighbours and sometimes automatically when the 999 call for an ambulance is made. It is very important for police officers and the coroner's officer to explain to parents why they are there, for most parents will never have had to cope with a sudden death and will have no idea of the legal procedures involved.

Thankfully police involvement is one area where improvements have taken place in recent years, thanks largely to education on the part of the FSID and more preparation in police training, but there is no room for complacency. Like hospital emergency staff, no policeman or policewoman should be expected to attend a cot death without thorough training beforehand. If police recruits find that such training is not available, then it is in their own interests to request it, for the trauma involved in a cot death should never be underestimated.

At one time it was not uncommon to see a police car race to the scene and for prying neighbours to see uniformed officers rushing into the house. This tended to fan rumours of an unnatural death, with all the attendant heartache that this could cause to the bereaved family concerned. Some officers, aware that suspicious deaths do exist, tended to be grossly insensitive in their approach. One distraught father was made to re-enact the whole scene of his baby's death using his baby's favourite teddy as a substitute. Parents have been known to be cross-questioned in a callous and hostile manner at the police station whilst still in deep shock, not knowing where their dead baby had been taken and wanting only to be allowed to go and give a cuddle and say goodbye.

Involvement by the police and the coroner's officer can make parents feel immediately guilty that they have in some way caused their baby's death without knowing how. It is useful to remember that, whilst the police and the coroner's officer have a duty to look for the very occasional cases of unnatural death, they are also there to protect all innocent parents by exonerating them.

The police have a vital duty to perform and when they arrive on the scene they are not able to know whether the death has been a natural one or not, but how they handle the situation can have a profound affect on the parents and can greatly help or hinder their ability to cope and recover. It is all too easy to prejudge and leap to wrong conclusions. With increased awareness and knowledge of the sudden infant death syndrome, instances of callousness and hostility on the part of the police have decreased and they are being encouraged to regard such deaths as natural cot deaths unless and until a post-mortem reveals any evidence to the contrary. They are also being encouraged to attend the scene out of uniform, to try and arrange for a woman police officer to be available and to treat the bereaved parents with understanding and compassion.

Being active is always easier, and if there is any sign of life in the baby at all, then police officers who arrive are able to undertake immediate efforts at resuscitation, sometimes with success. It is attending after death has already occurred that police officers tend to find most difficult.

Like other professionals involved, police officers, too, are deeply affected by a baby's sudden death. Doctors are trained to heal and a cot death faces them with a situation that can't be healed. Police officers are trained to maintain the law and to detect crime and a cot death faces them with a situation where a fundamental law (that someone who is apparently healthy does not just suddenly die) has been devastatingly broken and yet where there is no crime and therefore no one to arrest and bring to justice. All our natural instincts are to blame someone or something; we need to channel our anger and grief in this way – no wonder that, in the absence of any other source, God often gets the blame! Police officers are figures of authority but they are also human, often with young children of their own. Witnessing a cot death is a very distressing experience and, like others involved, they should be given an opportunity later to off-load some of the emotional burden which they carry by being allowed to express their feelings to a partner, colleague or independent but understanding listener.

The minister of religion

One of the most powerful emotions following a cot death is that of anger, sheer helpless rage that our baby is dead and we are unable to bring him or her back to life. Since for believers God is the giver of life, this rage may very often direct itself against God. It may lead bereaved families to reject their former faith or paradoxically it may lead to an increase in faith because death is such a very primal experience which puts us in touch both with ourselves and with what is eternal.

Those with a religious faith often suffer added strain when their baby dies. One such friend, Marilyn, expressed the dilemma well: 'In many ways grief is harder to cope with as a Christian. I knew that God loved me and could say that with complete assurance. I knew that he was upholding me and that many people were praying for me. Because of all this I imagined that my grief would pass quickly and easily. I was not prepared for the length and severity of the normal grief process. I often felt that I was failing God when I wasn't behaving the way I 'ought' to. I was angry and didn't understand why God had taken Luke, but I didn't feel I could express that anger. I've since realized that God made me with the ability to love and must therefore have made me with the capacity to grieve.'

Like the other professionals, the minister of religion has a potentially very important role to play following a cot death. In the survey of 713 unexpected infant deaths, almost half the parents cited ministers as the most valuable source of help, secondary only to family and friends. Often ministers of religion have very astute insights into the effects of grief because of the very nature of their work.

Even if parents are not regular church attenders and feel hesitant about asking a minister to call in case they are given a sermon about God at a time when they feel least able to accept it, such parents should not hesitate to contact their local minister because he can be of great support. On a practical level, he can explain the procedures involved when arranging the funeral and cremation or burial and on an emotional level he can give valuable counsel. He can only help if you let him, though.

Following Elizabeth's death I was visited by a minister of the Church of England. I did not know him because my occasional visits to church at that time had been to the Methodist church attended by friends. The minister was kind and gentle and at least talked about Elizabeth's death, a subject I had already discovered to be taboo by most people. We made stilted and polite conversation but at that time I couldn't begin to talk about what was crashing chaotically round in my mind. I had always believed in God. Because the twins had been born on a Sunday and had survived the early dangers of prematurity, I had felt them to be in some way blessed. I had prayed for their survival and they *had* survived. The name Elizabeth means 'consecrated to God' and I'd known this when we had chosen it. But I had prayed so hard while she'd lain on that hall carpet receiving resuscitation and she had not been restored to me.

Phrases from childhood mocked me. 'Only believe', 'Ask and it shall be given unto you.' Jairus's daughter had been brought back to life. I *had* believed and I *had* asked, but she had not been given unto me, she'd been taken away and my sense of anger and rejection were too deep for me even to begin to recognize. If God had loved me he would not have taken Elizabeth from me. The logical conclusion was that he did *not* love me, that Elizabeth's death must be punishment for some appalling sin I was not even aware of having committed. 'Whom God loveth, he chasteneth' – all right, perhaps I could convince myself that he *did* love me and was doing a fine job of chastening me, but what about Pat . . . and Rebecca . . . and Mary, and our families? What had they ever done to deserve the imposition of such grief upon them? What about Elizabeth herself? Nothing could make her death right. To have life given and then to have it snatched away when the whole of it lay ahead – that couldn't be right.

'The Lord giveth and the Lord taketh away, blessed be the name of the Lord.' I couldn't accept it. *Why?* *Why* had he given, only to take away? It was five years later that a Christian friend, Chris, advised me: 'You must give her to God. With all your grief – you must give them both to God,' and I realized a truth. Grief is not only supremely self-centred, it is also possessive. I still wanted Elizabeth and I still wanted my grief; they were mine. And then thankfully, for me, the problem resolved itself. It was not that God had taken Elizabeth, simply that he had been there to receive her when she went. A phrase from schooldays came back to me, from a poem by Wilfred Owen about soldiers going 'over the top' into battle in the First World War: 'Some say God caught them even before they fell.' I had never doubted Elizabeth's place in heaven. Now at last I could see that she hadn't been taken, she had been received.

For those who have already heard it, the following will probably seem clichéd, but it moved me and helped me when I first heard it. I don't suppose my memory is fully accurate, but the story as I remember it is that a woman dies, goes to heaven and then looks back at her life. There are two sets of footprints running side by side, hers and God's, until the various crises in her life are reached and passed. At those times only one set of footprints is visible, so she turns to God angrily and demands: 'Why did you desert me when I needed you most?' 'Ah no,' says God, 'I never deserted you – those are the times when I carried you.'

It seems to me that the subject of religion is almost as taboo these days as the subject of death. Everyone's so afraid of offending people about their particular beliefs that they avoid the topic altogether. Well, I've offered this for what it's worth. At the time of Elizabeth's death it would have been too soon to apply to me and it may never apply to you, but the insight of God as supportive and loving and receiving instead of as punishing and snatching away has been of profound help to me and the years since Elizabeth's death have seen me move from a very deep sense of rejection and hurt to the point where I now feel very aware of God's presence and support.

Perhaps, at the end of this very long chapter, it may give comfort to other bereaved parents if I recount an experience that happened to me a few days after the twins were born. At the time I thought that it was an experience unique to myself, but I have since heard other people relate something similar. I can't explain it, I simply offer it in case it helps.

When the twins were born they were seven weeks premature and in 1979 special care had not reached the level of success it now enjoys. When I asked if they would survive I was told: 'Give them a week. If they live through the first week they've got a good chance.' They were upstairs in the hospital block, in the Special Care Baby Unit. I was two floors below them in the general maternity ward, willing them to live. I felt that if I let go at all, they would die, so I virtually did not sleep, spending as much time with them as I was allowed and spending the remainder of my time lying in the ward trying to send telepathic messages to them that they must hold on and pull through. My bed was very close to the huge ward light, which was kept on for the benefit of the other mothers, who had to feed and change their babies through the night. Consequently, with all the noise and the light, sleep was almost impossible. After about five days I was also emotionally exhausted. Pat designed a home-made eye mask for me to shade me from the glare of the ward light and that night I attempted to sleep.

I dreamt that I was in a tunnel and at the end of it was a light so stunningly bright as to be indescribable. A child was leading me through the tunnel and I was only too happy to follow because I knew that at the end, if I turned left, I would cease to be a separate entity and would be totally absorbed into the brilliant light and become part of it and one with it. I was almost two-thirds of the way there when I heard myself saying: 'I'm sorry, I can't. I've got to go back, my family's back there and they need me.' The child went on alone and I returned. I woke sobbing and drenched with sweat. I was downstairs wearing Pat's eye mask. Mary was upstairs, wearing a mask because of her phototherapy treatment. My first thought was: 'She's died' and I rushed upstairs to her. It was 3 a.m. in the morning and the night staff were startled to say the least when I came hurtling into the Unit and dashed to Mary's cot. Maureen (who was a lovely nurse) cried: 'Mrs Murphy, whatever are you doing here at this time of night?' I couldn't tell her, I was too overcome with relief to find that Mary was still breathing. I then checked Elizabeth as well and found that both were perfectly all right.

Feeling very foolish, I returned to the ward, trying to make sense of what had happened. I wondered if the child who had led me could have been our first daughter, who had died at birth five years previously. The dream worried me deeply at the time, but since both the twins seemed fine I blamed the whole incident on sheer emotional exhaustion. After Elizabeth's sudden death twelve weeks later, inevitably I looked upon it in a new light. Premonition? Advance warning via our first child, or maybe via Elizabeth herself

– did she know already and did she try and tell me? In all honesty I don't know, but whatever the source of the experience, I felt very powerfully that it had given me a glimpse and therefore a very reassuring proof of the afterlife/heaven/oneness, whatever term seems most applicable since all are man-made words. This glimpse comforted me greatly afterwards. I knew that not only were my first baby and Elizabeth both part of the brilliant light but that I could become so as well, at the appropriate time. For anyone struggling with the bleak possibility that their baby has vanished into a void, a nothingness, I hope that the reassurance which I was given may be of help.

8

Another Baby?

When a subsequent baby may not be possible

For a chapter which is concerned with the prospect of another baby, it may seem strange to begin by considering those families for whom another baby can never be possible, but sadly this is the case for many cot-death parents and it is a reality which has to be faced, worked through and, if possible, resolved. In some instances mothers may have had to undergo a hysterectomy since last giving birth and although these mothers know that they will no longer be able to bear another child of their own, coming to terms with such knowledge can take a long time and be very painful. Couples who have separated since the death of their baby may feel, together with single-parent families, that they are facing a bleak future, because at such a time it is very difficult to imagine ever having a new relationship or another baby. Of course, for these parents circumstances may change. In time they may become reconciled to their previous partners, or they may meet new partners and make a fresh start – the possibility is always there.

As has been mentioned earlier, it is known that the higher the number of previous babies in the family, the greater the risk of a cot death becomes. Thus it is quite often the case that parents, who had thought that their families were complete, may have undergone vasectomy or some form of female sterilization before the totally unexpected death of their baby, and these parents face great stress and heartsearching. Although reversals are sometimes possible, the procedure can take time, be expensive if carried out privately and may lead to deep disappointment since success is by no means guaranteed. Nowadays doctors seem more reluctant to sterilize until the existing baby is over 1 year old, but tragedies do still happen and it seems immensely unfair that those parents who thought that they were acting responsibly by undergoing sterilization should find themselves facing the extra heartache of knowing that future conception may not be possible.

Provided you feel emotionally strong enough to press your case, don't just assume that the situation can't be changed. Depending on which method of sterilization was used, it is worth asking the surgeon concerned or searching to find a sympathetic surgeon willing to attempt a reversal operation if there is even a slight hope of success.

When a subsequent baby is possible

For those parents fortunate enough to be able to contemplate having another baby, the issue still remains a difficult one because so many conflicting emotions are involved. By all means consult others, seek advice, listen to what experts and other parents have to say, but ultimately it is a decision which only you as a couple can make. Of course, ideally you will both feel the same, whether you choose to remain without another child or whether you opt to try for another baby. Since this is not an ideal world, however, you may well find yourselves facing a situation where one of you wants a subsequent baby whilst the other disagrees. As always, good communication will help and if you can try and explain your feelings to each other it may prevent future hurts and resentments. It is a situation where compromise is not possible, since either you have another baby or you don't, but it is worth remembering that feelings and attitudes can alter with time. In our own case, because we had a twin daughter we waited five years before deciding to try and have another baby and I think that we were right to give ourselves time to heal, but I do know that for many parents the prospect of waiting for any length of time would simply be unbearable because the desire for a baby to love is so very strong.

Allowing time to heal

If it feels right to go ahead and try to conceive as soon as possible, then you must be true to your instincts, although it would be wise to avoid having a new baby on or around the anniversary of the previous baby's birth or death as this can be such a stressful time. It is worth bearing in mind, however, that rapid successive pregnancies are known to increase the risk of cot death and that a mother's body apparently takes up to two years to recover fully from the effects of pregnancy and childbirth. Since so many cot-death babies die under the age of 6 months, conceiving another baby quickly will mean that this recovery time will not be possible and complications may result. The miscarriage rate for mothers wanting a subsequent baby does seem to be ironically high, as does the rate for failing to conceive at all for a while. Perhaps it may be the case that while our hearts are sending us one message, our bodies are sending another – that we need time to heal physically as well as emotionally. Whilst it would be quite wrong to assume that a next pregnancy will be doomed to failure, if you can prepare yourself for the possibility that a subsequent baby may take some time in arriving, this may reduce the acute disappointment felt if success if not immediate. (It is also worth remembering that a rapid subsequent pregnancy can carry a higher risk of cot death (see Chapter 1).

Parents who lose a second, third or fourth baby have the reassurance of knowing that they have already succeeded before in their parenting role. Being aware that they have proved themselves capable of bringing a child safely through babyhood can give them the courage to have a subsequent baby following a cot death, but for first-time parents the cot death shatters all their confidence as parents, making them feel total failures and unworthy of parent-hood, despite the fact that cot deaths can neither be predicted nor prevented. A mother who gave up her job during late pregnancy can feel completely lost when her baby dies unexpectedly. From having two defined roles – working woman and then mother – she suddenly has neither and life can seem very aimless and empty indeed. Cut off from her previous work colleagues and friends and psychologically barred from any friends she may have made at antenatal classes or baby clinics since she no longer 'qualifies' for what brought them together, she is faced with the prospect of a silent house which may seem to mock her with its constant reminders of the baby who should still be with her. Even if the job which she did previously can be made available again, the depth and intensity of the experiences which she has undergone since leaving, encompassing both birth and death, can make it seem a pointless and irrelevant exercise to her now. No wonder the option of another baby seems a very attractive one, even on the days when such an option fills her with fear and even though she has not yet allowed herself the opportunity to grieve fully for her baby who died.

In an article in the *British Medical Journal* in 1979, entitled 'Inhibition of mourning by pregnancy', Emanuel Lewis pointed out that a bereaved pregnant woman 'has conflicting and paradoxical needs to think and feel intensely both about the new life and the dead. She opts for her live baby and mourning is interrupted, it is often too difficult while she nurtures her new baby, and is often impossible to resume later. Unresolved mourning may be reacti-vated in pathological forms by later events . . . Strong feelings about the loss may be suppressed, leading to a sense of being emotionally cut off; and this may impair the tie to the new baby.'

This does not mean that such an outcome is inevitable. Please don't think that here is yet another stick of guilt with which to beat yourself as you long for another baby, simply that his comments are worth bearing in mind when making any decision concerning a future pregnancy.

It is easy for outsiders to jump willingly into the trap of believing that a new baby will heal all the hurt, replace the dead baby and make everyone happy again. Bereaved parents are not so easily or so willingly fooled, but there is still a temptation for them to think that a new baby will make everything right again and take away the unbearable ache inside. Some even delude themselves that the new baby will be a reincarnation of the baby who died and may maintain this delusion even if the new baby proves to be of a different sex. Such parents need to be helped to face the reality of their previous baby's death so that they can enjoy their new baby in his or her own right.

When Elizabeth died we were in the unusual position of having a ready-made baby in her twin Mary to receive our care and our love. I shall always be grateful for that, but there was a price to pay. Being given no chance to mourn and to adjust meant that much of Mary's babyhood is now a blank to me. We lived through it, we even had moments of happiness, but we must have been functioning on auto-pilot much more than I had realized, for I have very few memories of the traditional milestones such as first tooth, first words and first walk.

Having Mary didn't remove the longing for Elizabeth and at times I felt an overwhelming desire to become pregnant and have another baby, but I also knew that none of us was feeling emotionally strong enough to cope. Pat was very definite that he could not bear to risk going through such trauma and heartache again and so I tried to fill the gap that I was feeling so much by becoming as busy as possible. I went to night-classes, became qualified as a playgroup supervisor, ran one playgroup and then established and ran another. I joined various committees. I even renewed a childhood love by buying a beautiful palomino horse and giving her the love I was wanting to give to an absent baby and I learnt what was for me an inescapable truth – there is no substitute for a baby, that particular gap could not be filled no matter how busy I tried to be.

I wasn't trying to replace Elizabeth, I did know that she was irreplaceable, but the deep aching wouldn't go away. I had the sense not to try to nag or pressurize Pat into the thought of another baby because I knew that, for us to cope successfully, we would both have to be in full agreement. Thankfully, time provided the solution. When Mary was 5 and at school all day and all reminders of babyhood had long since gone, Pat unexpectedly agreed to my tentative suggestion of another baby. The joy of an immediate conception was promptly crushed by a very early miscarriage – a common problem, but no less distressing because of it, and enough to destroy my fragile self-confidence and cause temporary self-doubt and depression again. Thankfully, once my periods had returned to normal, pregnancy became a possibility again; Christopher was conceived and he was born safely on 30 September 1985. If it is of any help to know this, it is a decision which we have never, even for a single moment, regretted. Despite the anxieties and fears, he has brought us more joy than we ever thought possible.

The next baby

Friends and family want happiness for you, so it is natural that they tend to say: 'How wonderful for you that you're pregnant, you must be so happy' – not so much a statement, more a command, a plea for you to assure them that you *are* happy because your pain is to some degree their pain, too. It would be more honest and more sensitive if family members and friends could say: 'I'm very glad you're pregnant, but I can understand it if you're having very mixed feelings about the coming baby and if you don't feel able to enjoy being pregnant the way you did last time.' Don't be afraid to mention the previous pregnancy and baby. The one guarantee you can have is that the mother won't have forgotten! Speaking about the previous baby instead of pretending that he or she never existed can give the mother a much-needed opening to talk about her memories and her grief as well as her fears and hopes for the coming child.

The whole procedure of antenatal care inevitably stirs memories and raises comparisons. GPs and antenatal staff need to be sensitive to this and phrase their questions carefully during the first check-up. 'Is this your first baby?' can leave mothers with the unenviable task of having to say: 'No, this is our second, our first baby died in a cot death.' Having the subject raised by someone else is very much easier than having to state it oneself, especially during the emotional early stages of pregnancy. Accurate records can do much to help prepare GPs and hospital staff appropriately and thereby alleviate the expectant mother of a difficult problem. Mothers are usually immensely grateful when staff say: 'I know from your notes that your last baby died in a cot death. I'm very sorry. I can guess how much both your last baby and this new baby must mean to you and this can't be an easy time for you.'

Many mothers when embarking on a subsequent pregnancy experience strong feelings of disloyalty to the child who has died and can feel very guilty if they find themselves enjoying the pregnancy and looking forward to the prospect of a new baby to love. Such feelings are natural but they are unnecessary, for the love of their previous baby does not die when the baby dies, and the baby, even though absent, will always remain a valued member of the family. This is also what the new baby should become – a valued member in his or her own right. Great care must be taken not to idealize the baby who died. Once they are old enough to understand, subsequent children will need to be told very sensitively about the death of their older brother or sister, for it is a difficult knowledge with which to come to terms. 'Am I only second best, then, just a replacement and not wanted for myself?' Such thoughts may not be expressed by subsequent children, but they may well be felt. Take time to reassure your subsequent children that they are greatly loved and valued. Competing with older brothers or sisters is difficult at the best of times. Trying to compete with a dead brother or sister may well prove impossible and very damaging to their own sense of self-worth and self-esteem unless parents can give constant reassurance of their love.

Coping with anxiety

For all couples fortunate enough to be able to have another baby, it is inevitable that they will feel very anxious at times, both during the pregnancy and after the birth. As mentioned before, cot death damages self-confidence and it certainly removes all guarantees. Since it has happened once, there is always the fear that it may happen again. Statistically such a fear has little foundation. Of every 500 subsequent babies born to cot-death parents, at least 496 can expect to survive without any problems. The risk of recurrence is no greater than the risk of having a stillbirth in the general population, but this knowledge is sometimes of little comfort to cot-death parents. After all, their previous baby was the one in 500, why shouldn't their next baby be the exception to the rule as well? At the times when panic-attacks threaten, it can be very helpful to talk to other cot-death parents who have had subsequent babies, because they won't patronize or give uninformed and therefore unconvincing reassurances. They are in the very special position of being able to say: 'Yes, we understand, we've been there too; hold on and ride it out because such panic-attacks are perfectly natural and they honestly do pass.'

We experienced moments of intense anxiety during Christopher's first year. What surprised and pleased us was how much we were able nevertheless to enjoy his babyhood. We had expected an endurance test, a symbolic holding of breath until the greatest danger period had passed, but instead we found ourselves able to appreciate every stage. Awareness that a future was by no means assured made us in a very real way 'live each day as if 'twere the last', not in any morbid sense but in an intense grasping and holding of present happiness.

CONI – Care of the Next Infant

Hopefully all parents embarking on a subsequent pregnancy should soon be able to take advantage of the scheme known as CONI – care of the next infant, which has evolved as a result of the Infant Home Surveillance Research Project. This project was funded by the Foundation for the Study of Infant Deaths and launched in 1980 to provide and evaluate support for cot-death families coping with a subsequent baby. Initially the project undertook a pilot study of 100 families using randomized equipment (either an apnoea monitor or weighing scales) combined with daily symptom diaries and weekly visits from the health visitor. The project proved successful and in 1984 evolved into a multicentre study and expanded from five centres in 1984 to twenty-three centres in 1988, involving twenty-seven health authorities.

The study was welcomed by families despite the fact that a small number of unexpected infant deaths did occur where either monitors or weighing scales or both were in use at the time. The study resulted in the establishment of a protocol for support known as CONI, which the Foundation decided to offer to health authorities to assist them in providing care for subsequent babies. The Foundation agreed to make funds available on a loan basis, the loan to be repaid from locally raised funds (usually raised by the nearest parent group). It also agreed to finance initial costs such as stationery and travelling expenses for the first three years or until twenty cases were being handled by each centre, with centres thereafter being responsible for their own costs.

Methods of support for individual families

For CONI to work, the Foundation recognized that support would be needed from paediatricians, nurse managers, co-ordinators, health visitors and general practitioners. It was felt that the following areas of support would be most appropriate:

(1) Regular weekly contact in the home, with an informed health visitor, the support of a knowledgeable general practitioner and ready access to an interested paediatrician.
(2) Symptom diaries, completed by parents and discussed with health visitors, to allow parents to express anxiety about illness in the whole family and facilitate health education.
(3) Weight charts. It was felt that all babies on the scheme should have their weights recorded on the Sheffield Weight Chart at regular intervals.
(4) Weighing – daily or regular weighing of the baby in the home by parents, with the weights recorded on to Sheffield Weight Charts.
(5) Apnoea monitoring, with provision of an apnoea monitor for the baby and the choice of which type to use to be left to local users.
(6) Measurement of environmental temperature. It was felt that regular recording could be useful, since both heat and cold can be dangerous in some circumstances.

It was agreed that all families would be offered (1), (2) and (3) above and in addition parents would be encouraged to use one other method of surveillance, in appropriate cases perhaps using all three of (4), (5) and (6), plus other methods if recommended by the paediatrician involved.

With these aims in view, the Foundation appointed a national CONI organizer, with regional organizers to be appointed as and when appropriate. By the summer of 1989 twenty-five centres were already in operation, working to the following guidelines.

Following cot death

(1) All parents should be offered appropriate bereavement support, plus an opportunity to talk with a paediatrician following their child's death, including counselling and preliminary plans for the care of a next infant.
(2) Full details of the cot-death child should be compiled, including a detailed history from the family, a post-mortem report and background information from the general practitioner and health visitor.

Care of the Next Infant

(1) To avoid the risk of cot-death families being unidentified or overlooked, sources of referral in early pregnancy should include obstetricians and midwives in antenatal clinics, plus GPs undertaking full obstetric care, plus health visitors, family GPs and community midwives in contact with the families.
(2) Parents should be interviewed during the pregnancy by both the paediatrician at the hospital and the local co-ordinator at their home, with the first contact taking place early in the pregnancy and the second contact about two months before the expected date of confinement, in order to discuss and select appropriate methods of support.
(3) A suitable foolproof system of notification of the baby's birth should be developed so that the co-ordinator can ensure that CONI support is offered without delay.
(4) All babies should be examined by the paediatrician before discharge from hospital. As a routine investigation for siblings of SIDS babies, a urine sample should be analyzed for signs of MCAD deficiency (known to be the cause of SIDS in about 7 per cent of cases, see Chapter 1 p. 9), plus other investigations undertaken if appropriate.
(5) The family GP should be kept informed and involved throughout all procedures.
(6) Arrangements should be made for health visitors to visit the families on a weekly basis, as this has been found to be of most

help to families with subsequent babies. On average, one health visitor is likely to care for a subsequent child once in three years.

(7) Midwives should do all they can to identify mothers early in pregnancy and support them in the newborn period, hopefully launching the CONI programme immediately after birth and assisting in the task of collecting urine samples for analysis.

(8) FSID local parent groups should be asked to assist in identifying cot-death families, in raising funds for locally used equipment and in befriending for as long as they are needed.

(9) All parents should be shown how to resuscitate before the subsequent baby is born. (In the Sussex area an excellent scheme exists known as Heartguard. Trained volunteers undertake two hours of teaching the resuscitation of both adults and babies and they provide working dummy models on which groups of interested learners can practise what they have just been taught. The volunteers are aware that practising resuscitation on a very likelife dummy baby is a most stressful and emotional undertaking for cot-death parents, but the experience helps to rebuild self-confidence. It is a skill which cot-death parents hope never to have to use, but knowing that they have acquired it gives immense reassurance.)

Using monitors and scales

I have gone into some detail in outlining CONI in order to enable parents who are expecting a subsequent baby to reach an informed decision about whether they would like to participate in the scheme. Hopefully the details will also enable interested health professionals to learn more about the scheme and perhaps initiate it in their area if it is not already in operation.

From a practical point of view, all cot-death parents have to work out what suits them best. As with grieving, there are no right or wrong responses and what suits one couple may not necessarily suit another. The current options are few: to join the CONI scheme (if it is available in the area) or to go it alone; to try and care for your baby as if the cot death had never happened (a very difficult aim to achieve); to give in to 'cot watching' but forgo the use of a monitor or scales as a source of reassurance; or to use a monitor or scales or both. Since the pros and cons of monitors and scales have already been analyzed in Chapter 1 (see pp. 12–14), the only decision for you to make here is whether they would be of help to you in caring for your subsequent baby. It is an area where opinions differ widely. I have spoken to couples who found the use of a monitor very reassuring, others who relied upon scales to give them tangible proof of their baby's steady progress, and others who felt that they would prefer to cope without any external 'props' and who then went on to cope very successfully. It is yet another potential source of strain in a relationship, because what may be right for one of the parents may upset or distress the other.

We were very lucky where Christopher was concerned, because we were both adamant that we needed the reassurance of an apnoea monitor. We chose the Graseby model and while being well aware of its limitations, we found it of immense help. To be able to stand outside the room where Chistopher was sleeping in his pram or his cot and to hear the regular 'click-click' recording each breath was very welcome indeed and it meant that we could then enter the room with confidence. Yes, we had a number of times when the alarm went off, but this never made us panic because we were able to tell ourselves that it probably only meant that the micropore tape holding the small pad in place on his tummy had come loose. Usually this proved to be the case. On about four occasions I could find no explanation for the alarm, but in each case its sound had made Christopher stir, so that I never faced the dreaded sight of a baby lying too quiet and still. I don't know why those alarms happened. Perhaps he went for too long without breathing and perhaps the sound of the alarm jolted him into breathing normally again. There is no way of knowing, but I do know that I trusted the monitor, despite its limitations, and was very grateful for its presence.

Much has been said both for and against the use of monitors, but really the situation is very simple. At present, there is no scientific proof that monitors save lives and babies have been known to die even whilst being monitored. They are not a guarantee against cot death, but on the other hand they can be a source of reassurance. The decision is one for the parents alone to make, not for doctors or experts. It is the parents who have experienced their baby's death, not outsiders. They alone should have the option of accepting or refusing the provision of a monitor. The role of doctors is to explain clearly the advantages and limitations of such monitors, not to make a decision about whether or not they should be issued. The parents will soon discover whether using one brings them reassurance or increases the stress which they will already be feeling. If a monitor helps, use it. If it doesn't, then don't.

I do sometimes wonder what effect the monitor had on Christopher. He is an extremely alert and active child who does not seem to need much sleep and who has always been a very light sleeper, still waking and coming through to our bedroom in the night at the age of 3½. Would this have been his personality anyway, or did being abruptly woken out of deep sleeps as a baby by the alarm going off have some effect on his sleeping pattern? It is perhaps a point to bear in mind if choosing to use a monitor. We certainly don't regret our decision; it enabled us to enjoy his babyhood and, despite my worries that we might become too dependent on it and be unable to stop using it, Christopher weaned himself off the monitor quite naturally at the age of 10 months.

The aim of the Foundation is that all cot-death parents caring for a subsequent baby should, if they wish, have access either to a monitor or to weighing scales. It is an ambitious aim, for both are expensive, their effectiveness in saving lives is scientifically unproven and many doctors and paediatricians are reluctant to support their use, but the Foundation recognizes that, for many families, they supply much-needed support.

Weighing scales have certain advantages over monitors. They do not involve any procedure such as the strapping of a sensor pad to the baby's tummy, they are easy to use, require only a few minutes each day for the actual weighing and, through the recorded results, give visible proof that the baby is gaining weight and thriving. In addition, sudden weight losses mean that potential health problems can be recognized and dealt with very quickly. Daily weighing has been known to detect the very early stages of kidney infections and other potentially serious illnesses, since weight loss often precedes such illnesses and is instantly visible when the centile charts are used to map the baby's progress. Weighing scales can prove to be very useful but, as with monitors, the final decision about whether to use them should rest with the parents themselves, since they are the ones with greatest responsibility for the care of their subsequent baby and they are the ones who have to cope.

Think positive!

As outlined in Chapter 1, certain positive steps can be taken both before and during pregnancy to give any future baby the best start in life and reduce the risk of cot death. It is wise, for example, to avoid a rapid subsequent pregnancy, especially if the mother is very young and already has surviving children. It is worth ensuring that both partners are in the best possible health, that they avoid smoking and the use of drugs and unnecessary medicines and that they aim to achieve a summer conception which will lead to a springtime baby. If the mother can continue to avoid smoking and drugs (including barbiturates) after conception, maintain a good balanced diet, attend regularly for antenatal check-ups and allow herself plenty of rest, she will improve her chances of havng a full-term, full-weight, healthy baby, who will therefore be least at risk of cot death. That is an ideal and it is worth aiming to achieve in so far as home circumstances will allow, but of course it is not always possible and conception is not an exact science! We had hoped to have an early springtime baby, since February and March are statistically the safest months for birth as far as cot deaths are concerned. As mentioned before, however, that pregnancy ended in early miscarriage and what we achieved was an autumn baby, born at the end of September during the highest risk time of year (cot deaths peak at around Christmas time when the babies are about 3 months old). Our baby proved to be a boy and boys are known to be at slightly higher risk of cot death than girls, and he also tried to arrive ten weeks early (and premature babies are also known to be at higher risk). Thankfully prompt and efficient medical attention in hospital halted the premature labour and I was able to carry Christopher to full-term. What is worth bearing in mind is that, while it is sensible to try and load the dice in your future baby's favour, don't panic if events don't work out according to plan. Being a technically high-risk baby does *not* necessarily mean that cot death will occur. On the other hand, it makes sense to give any future baby the best possible chances of avoiding the risk of cot death and this includes avoiding crowded and germ-laden places during the first six months after birth if at all possible.

All of these above suggestions may leave you wondering whether you dare risk having another baby at all! Think positively. Not many babies are born in totally ideal circumstances and yet in the early 1980s in England and America, out of every 1,000 babies born alive 990 managed to survive their first year without mishap. Only 8 per 1,000 died from congenital conditions or severe infection and only 2 per 1,000 died in cot deaths. One hundred years ago the survival rate would have been 850 out of 1,000. Now it is 990 out of 1,000. There has never been a better or a safer time to have a baby. If you both want to do so, then go ahead, because your subsequent baby can bring you more happiness than you would ever have thought possible.

A Personal Conclusion

I finished writing this book in August 1989, within a month of the tenth anniversary of Elizabeth's death. On the morning that I did so, I then drove to the farm where I keep my lovely Arab mare Tizzy and we went for a canter through nearby Devil's Dyke, in Sussex. Tizzy is full of spirit, she has a joy of living which I value, having had so much of it crushed out of me by Elizabeth's death. It was a glorious morning with the sun shining and, as we cantered, the wind whipped tears to my eyes. Not far through the valley the ground became too hard for cantering any more, but even though we stopped, the tears didn't and I realized that I was crying in earnest – for myself, for Elizabeth, for all the tiny babies and young children who'd died, for their families and everyone touched by their tragic and baffling deaths. I cried from one end of the valley to the other and Tizzy, perhaps sensitive to my mood, walked along quietly, allowing me to grieve undisturbed.

Riding back along the ridge, I saw a magpie fly past – 'one for sorrow' – well, it would be, wouldn't it, I thought, but then I realized that life could be no other way, that if I was to let myself live fully then the numbers of magpies would always vary and at times would have to include 'one for sorrow' and at times 'two for joy'. Coming back along Dyke Lane, Tizzy and I saw three magpies foraging together in a field – 'three for a girl' – for Elizabeth, the little baby I still love and miss so much. Riding back quietly through the fields to the farm, I wondered if I would be allowed to see 'two for joy', but I didn't, life isn't as neat as that. It didn't matter. I knew by then that in the years since Elizabeth's death I had been able to see plenty of magpies in pairs, giving 'two for joy', when I had chosen to look for them, and that, provided I went on looking in the right places, I would continue to see them in the future.

Our children are not the ones we'd planned or expected and in a way that makes them all the more precious as a result. Having twins had been a wonderful surprise; losing Elizabeth a devastating shock. Had she lived, the influences on Rebecca and Mary would have been different from those which they have had to experience, yet we would not want to change them from the lovely children they have proved to be. Had Elizabeth lived, we would not now have

118

Christopher who brings us so much happiness. I wish she had lived, but I cannot regret what has followed from her death, nor all that it has taught us.

One of the overwhelming needs of many cot-death parents is the need to talk about their feelings and about the baby who has died. I set out to write this book as a way of helping you as bereaved parents and also those around you. Of course, if you've listened by reading the book then you've helped me, too.

Appendix 1

Information List

This list has been prepared by the Foundation for the Study of Infant Deaths, and is reproduced with their permission.

LEAFLETS	Written for	Contents
Information for parents following the Sudden and Unexpected Death of their Baby (1987)	Bereaved parents	Explains what little is known and what the post-mortem may show; answers the most usual questions and describes normal grief reactions; explains coroner's role and where to seek further help
Your Next Child	Formerly bereaved parents	Advice to help parents with their anxieties when contemplating, expecting or caring for a subsequent baby
When to Consult a Doctor about your Baby (Green Card)	New mothers (not only formerly bereaved parents)	Describes urgent, sometimes serious symptoms of illness in babies; gives infant-care guidance on feeding, crying, sleeping position and temperature
Support for parents Bereaved by an Unexpected Infant Death	Health professionals, enquirers, parent groups	Single sheet outlines parents' needs, the role of health professionals, and the information and support offered by the Foundation
Cot Death Check-list for GPs	General practitioners	Brief advice on immediate support needs of the family
Guidelines for Accident and Emergency Dept. (Orange Card)	Accident and Emergency Dept. staff	Brief guidelines for the management of a sudden infant death brought to hospital casualty departments

Newsletters	Parents, supporters of the Foundation, all enquirers	Published twice a year to keep parents and others on mailing list informed of research findings and activities of the Foundation
Cot Death Research and Support	Public	Research, support and information aims of the Foundation; financial needs
Appeals Leaflet	Public and contributors	Work of the Foundation; research for which funds are needed. Deed of Covenant form enclosed
BOOKS	*Written for*	*Contents*
Sudden Infant Death: Patterns, Puzzles and Problems, Jean Golding, Sylvia Limerick and Aidan McFarlane, Open Books, Beaumont House, New St, Wells, Somerset BA5 2LD	Paediatricians, family doctors, social workers, parents	Part I: Setting the scene Part II: Epidemiological studies Part III: Possible causes of Sudden Infant Death Part IV: Reactions to Death Part V: The Way Ahead? Glossary, References, Index
Cot Deaths, Jacquelynn Luben, Thorsons Publishers Ltd, Dennington Estate, Wellingborough, Northants NN8 2RQ	Parents and general reading	First-hand account from a mother who lost her baby daughter as a cot death. It offers clear advice on how to cope with the trauma and its aftermath
When a Baby Suddenly Dies: Cot Death – The Impact and Effects, Janet Deveson Lord, Hill of Content, Pub Co Pty Ltd, 86 Bourke St, Melbourne, Aust.	Parents, supporting services, health professionals	A complete resource book for those responding to the impact of cot death from a trained counsellor who lost a daughter as a cot death

| *Where's Jess?*, Joy and Mary Johnson, Centering Corp, Box 3367, Omaha, Nebraska 68103, USA | Bereaved parents and siblings | A picture book to help parents explain the death of the baby to other siblings, based on real family. |

ANNUAL REPORT AND ACCOUNTS	*Written for*	*Contents*
Annual Report and Accounts of FSID	Members of Foundation and supporters	Reviews scientific, support and information and fundraising activities, Chairman's and Treasurer's reports

LISTS	*Written for*	*Contents*
Reference list of Welfare and Health education articles	Health visitors, nurses and midwives, health students, doctors	Selected list of articles published in UK since 1971 relevant to the welfare and health educational aspects of the problem
List of Foundation's Research Projects	Doctors	Researcher's name; outlines objectives of each research project; gives references to published results

WEIGHT CHARTS	*Written for*	*Contents*
Sheffield *Centile* Weight Charts		New *centile* weight charts have been designed for infants in the first year of life, based upon measurements made at two-week intervals on 259 infants studied in Sheffield in the 1970s. The charts are on sale from the Foundation (which has been granted the copyright) and are available in two sizes:

INFORMATION LIST

	Parents	Envelope containing two A1-size *centile* weight charts (1 boy, 1 girl), weight chart instruction sheet, six symptom charts, general information and green card giving advice on signs and symptoms of illness in babies
	Health authorities	A3-size *centile* weight charts for boys and girls, plus instructions

VIDEO FILMS	Designed for	Contents
The US Dept of Health Education & Welfare films **You Are Not Alone** (30 mins)	Bereaved parents, health professionals	Portrays the reactions of several couples to a sudden infant death and is designed to help parents and professionals who are supporting newly bereaved families
After Our Baby Died (30 mins) These two films (above) are both on one video		Intends to arouse discussion about the counselling needs of bereaved parents and is meant to be introduced with a short talk about sudden infant deaths
A Call For Help (20 mins)	Police	This is a training film for police forces. It explains sudden death syndrome and examines the immediate handling of a natural sudden infant death
TV South Films **The Purple Line** (60 mins)	Public, health professionals and groups	Health-visitor surveillance of 'high risk' infants

My Beautiful Baby is Dead (20 mins)	as above	This shows the work of the Hampshire Parent Support Group

These two films
(above) are both on
one video

Leap for Life Film

I'm Sorry your Baby is Dead but I Can't Tell You Why (33 mins)	Health professionals, ambulance staff, police	Designed to help professionals understand the needs of bereaved parents. This is available for purchase from FSID, in VHS/BETA format at £25.00

All of these videos are available on VHS, BETA and SONY U-MATIC formats and may be borrowed from FSID for £3.00 each (to cover outgoing P&P) plus borrower paying return registered postage. Please book them in advance and return them as soon as you have finished with them.

Appendix 2

Useful Addresses

United Kingdom

The Foundation for the Study of Infant Deaths
35 Belgrave Square,
London, SW1X 8PS.
Tel: 01 235 1721/071 235 0965

The Compassionate Friends
6 Denmark Street,
Clifton,
Bristol, BS1 5DQ.
Tel: 0272 292778

Twins & Multiple Births Association (TAMBA)
Chairman (As from July 1989)
1 Victoria Place,
King's Park,
Stirling FK8 2QX.

The National Childbirth Trust
Alexandra House,
Oldham Terrace,
Acton, London W3 6NH.

Foresight (for advice prior to subsequent pregnancy)
The Old Vicarage,
Church Lane,
Witley,
Godalming,
Surrey GU8 5PN.
Tel: Wormley (0 42879) 4500

United States of America

National Sudden Infant Death Syndrome Foundation (NSIDSF)
Two Metro Plaza,
8200 Professional Place,
Suite 104,
Landover, MD 20857.
Tel: (800) 221-7437

National SIDS Clearing House
8201 Greensboro Drive,
Suite 600,
McLean - VA 22102.
Tel: (703) 821 8955

International Council for Infant Survival (ICIS)
2956 Eric Lane,
Dallas,
Texas 75234.

Australia

National SIDS Council of Australia
1227 Malvern Road,
Malvern,
Victoria 3144.
Tel: 3822 0766

Canada

Canadian Foundation for the Study of Infant Deaths
P.O. Box 190, Station R,
Toronto,
Ontario M49 329
Tel: (416) 483 4135

New Zealand

Cot Death Division
National Children's Health Research Foundation,
P.O. Box 28–177,
Auckland 5.

South Africa

Cot Death Society
P.O. Box 11306,
Vlaeberg 8012.

Cot Death Foundation (RSA)
34 Julia Street,
Birchleigh North,
Kempton Park 1619.

Appendix 3

When to Consult a Doctor about Your Baby

* *IF YOU THINK your baby is ill even without any obvious symptoms*
  CONTACT YOUR DOCTOR
* *IF YOUR BABY shows any of the following symptoms especially if he*
  has more than one
  YOUR DOCTOR would expect you to ask for advice

Always urgent

- a fit or convulsion, or turns blue or very pale
- quick, difficult or grunting breathing
- exceptionally hard to wake or unusually drowsy or does not seem to know you

Sometimes serious

- croup or a hoarse cough with noisy breathing
- cannot breathe freely through his nose
- cries in an unusual way or for an unusually long time or you think your baby is in severe pain
- refuses feeds repeatedly, especially if unusually quiet
- vomits repeatedly
- frequent loose motions especially if watery (diarrhoea)
  Vomiting and diarrhoea together can lead to excessive loss of fluid from the body and this may need urgent treatment
- unusually hot or cold or floppy

* *Even if you have consulted a doctor, health visitor or nurse, IF BABY is not improving or is getting worse, TELL YOUR DOCTOR AGAIN THE SAME DAY.*

Emergency action

Get medical help immediately

- contact your DOCTOR
- telephone for an AMBULANCE (dial 999) or
- take baby to a Hospital ACCIDENT or CASUALTY department

WHEN TO CONSULT A DOCTOR

While waiting for a doctor or ambulance to arrive:

If baby is not breathing

- stimulate baby by flicking the soles of his feet or picking him up
  If no response, begin RESUSCITATION through his mouth-and-nose
- place baby on his back on a table or other firm surface
- suck the baby's nose clear

If baby does not gasp or breathe:

- support the back of his neck, tilt his head backwards and hold his chin upwards
- open your mouth wide and breathe in
- seal your lips round his nose and mouth
- breathe GENTLY into his lungs until his chest rises
- remove your mouth to allow the air to come out and let his chest fall
- repeat gentle inflations a little faster than your normal breathing rate, removing your mouth after each breath
  Baby should begin to breathe within a minute or so

For a fit or convulsion

- lay your baby on his tummy with his head low and turned to one side
- clear his mouth and nose of any sick or froth
- if he is hot, cool by sponging his head with tepid water (just warm)

For a burn or scald

- put the burnt or scalded part immediately in clean cold water
- lightly cover the part with a very clean cloth or sterile dressing
- do not apply oil or ointments; do not prick blisters

For an accident

- give FIRST AID if you know how
- if your baby has swallowed pills, medicines or household liquids, *TAKE THE BOTTLE TO HOSPITAL AS WELL*

Index